BACK TO BARRON

ဆ • ભ

BACK TO BARRON

Life in the Heartland at Mid-Century

Daniel E. Van Tassel

NORTH STAR PRESS OF ST. CLOUD, INC.

St. Cloud, Minnesota

Printed in the United States of America

Published by
North Star Press of St. Cloud, Inc.
P.O. Box 451
St. Cloud, Minnesota 56302

northstarpress.com

info@northstarpress.com

Dedication

To the family, especially my sister Carole and my mother,
both now absent from the fold, and my father, a perfect
match for Chaucer's faithful parson,
and to all—

"Those dear hearts and gentle people
who live and love in my hometown."

Contents

All the sun long it was running, it was lovely, the hay
Fields high as the house, the tunes from the chimneys, it was air
And playing, lovely and watery
And fire green as grass.

—Dylan Thomas, from "Fern Hill" (1946)

ॐ • ॐ

Introduction

B ACK TO BARRON: *Life in the Heartland at Mid-Century* is both a memoir and a valentine. Written in a style ranging from the schoolmarmish to the colloquial, the book charms like an heirloom on the mantel or an album on the coffee table, there to recall good times past. It covers a time of transition in America. The use of horses as beasts of burden had not given way entirely to tractors and modern machinery on the farm. Milking machines were making their début, post-war industry was getting underway and expanding, fast-food franchises, little leagues, and parent-organized "play" were still in the offing. It was life in the slow lane. Pollution had not nightmared into the reality it would become a few decades later. The small town sat apart from the centers of crime and congestion, cities flexing their commercial muscles and offering haven to those who took shortcuts to possession and chose anonymity over responsibility. Instead, life in the rural Midwest offered elbow room. The sign on the way into Northfield, Minnesota sums it up: "City of cows, colleges, and contentment." While Barron didn't boast an institution of higher learning, the school system worked and children grew up learning by example and from textbooks and experience. Not paradise without the serpent, it nonetheless was a wonderful, wholesome time and place to be growing up.

The book is chock full of descriptions and anecdotes documenting what life was like growing up in small-town America at mid-century. In an authentic voice, the author chronicles the adventures and ruminations of a latter-day Tom Sawyer, capturing what distinguishes youth from age. Whether horsing around on a farm or taking a dip on a hot summer day, boys of the era lived life to the hilt. They rollicked and dreamed, registering the things that really matter along life's way. Episodes and pranks on the farm, sporting on the river, attending school, and wandering town streets and woods and meadows on the lookout for fun—it is a period piece yet what it tells is timeless, blending the unique and the universal. The book is humorous, at times poignant, and throughout unabashedly nostalgic.

— from an anonymous reader

ഗ • ൫

Horse Racing

A.O. Johnson farmed 180 acres near Birchwood, Wisconsin, a village more than a town, and, unlike Barron, not a county seat with a grand court house. A.O. belonged to that minority of mysterious folks who went by initials rather than given names. Referred to somewhat informally yet deferentially by church members as Pastor Van, my father was officially known as the Reverend P.E. Van Tassel. Only our family, relatives, and closest friends were acquainted with the fact that he had been christened Prosper Ellsworth, his middle name also my namesake. Those really close to Dad, our aunts and uncles and my parents' old friends, called him Prop. The next sphere of familiarity authenticated their closeness by calling him Van. For the record, however, he was P.E. The initials and his ministerial garb assured him a place among the mysterious. Little Rodney Olson, whose family lived in a yellow house right next to First Lutheran, which edifice stood across the street from our two-story brick parsonage, was in awe of my dad. One Saturday afternoon in September, pointing his finger in the direction of the outside stairs leading to Dad's office which entered directly into the sacristy, Rodney announced to the older kids playing tag in the churchyard, "God lives up there!" He missed the mark a bit, but the focus of his reverence was on target.

Dad's mother, Nell, had a penchant for choosing aristocratic sounding names, labels that had potential to inspire or embarrass. His two sisters bore names reflecting the heavens and history: Stella and Genieve. His six brothers included Sherman, Evan, Beltram Noble, Chester, Earl, and Sterling. It puzzled me, this rogue strain of secularism that caused Gramma Van to eschew biblical names for her children, she being a devout Lutheran. I remember her as a reader of devotional booklets, an elderly woman who bore no nonsense from us kids and yet warmed up to us when she served tea and toast. Every day was regarded as Sunday, though we could observe that she got a tad sterner on the Lord's Day. Clearly, naming children was not a frivolous act. She held that parents could influence their children's destiny in part by how well they named them.

While it was not uncommon, under certain circumstances or at particular occasions, for persons to be addressed by their initials, the majority practice is to go by the first name. Some individuals are popularly known by their middle name, another cranny in which to deposit a secret. Then, too, a boy's middle name could be summoned as a link to join the first and last name at those times when the person addressing the boy was angry with the boy for a very good reason, the boy having committed a heinous, momentarily unforgivable act. When, for instance, I was caught in the act of hitting a neighbor girl and jerking a four-leaf clover out of her hand, shouting "It's mine, dummy!" Mother intervened sharply: "Why, Daniel Ellsworth Van Tassel!"

Nicknames are another story. Some nicknames are like scars and recall bad times. They persist as a form of teasing. Others are earned like badges of honor, as is the case with the naming of Native American children. A nickname doesn't have to humiliate, but nearly every one I can think of encapsulates a living joke. In Barron nicknames were mostly punitive, tantamount to life sentences, keeping their bearers in purgatory. Gloria Stoneberg was banished with Snotnose. Maynard

Morgan bore the tattoo of Chink. One of the Paulson boys literally never outgrew Peewee. Dubbed so by his brothers, his nickname stuck. I reckoned he had no choice but to stay small and remain true to the identity established by the handle he went by. He didn't fuss about it at all but cheerfully went on with his life and accepted what his growth hormones also had acquiesced to. Roger Turgeson's brother Don, who like my brother was one year older, failed second grade and sat as a twin in the same classroom with Roger and me for the rest of our school days. That's the explanation behind his being called Dope. Eugene Elkin innocuously answered to the alias Moe, a nickname representative of the non-derisive category. A nickname of that ilk is more or less interchangeable with the first name. A skinny youth, I maintained the title Noodle for a year or so. But somehow it didn't really take, even though I remained slim. Nicknames are more stigmatic than initials, though there are exceptions.

Around Barron a few people stood out for their identification by initials. Take E.B. Swenson. Folks never knew his actual first and middle names. Nor did his Hillsdale parishioners know whether his house calls were related to his avocation of insurance agent or to the fact that he was an ordained clergyman. When E.B. came knocking on your door, was he about to give a pitch for Jesus or was he bent on worldly concerns? A person didn't know what to expect. But one thing for sure, he made one pay attention to what could happen upon one's demise. Better be prepared. It was either life insurance or assurance of eternal bliss. E.B. was vigilant. But his vocation, not his initials and what they stood for, was the subject in question.

A.O. Johnson was an enigma. No one had ever known or, it was assumed, would ever learn what his legal names were. Not even grownups. I suppose the pastor who baptized him solemnly pronounced the infant's initials, after saying "thee," and went right on to conclude the ceremony with the sonorous words, "in the name of the Father, Son, and Holy Ghost." Everyone present must have been on tenterhooks. Probably attendance was at an all-time high that morning service, the

3

congregation of Scandinavian faithful hoping to have light shed on the dark secret of Baby A.O. As part of the conspiracy, the church bulletin that Sunday upheld the mystery behind little A.O. Nobody, not even A.O., blabbed.

I take guilty pride in having discovered the origin of A.O., a piece of gnostic information I happened on to when visiting A.O.'s farm one summer when I was nine or ten. My brother Phil and I had been abandoned there for several days. Mom and Dad had gone vacationing up to Lake of the Woods with big Mag Hansen and his jolly, equally hefty wife to catch oodles of fish and swat millions of mosquitos. Our three sisters, meanwhile, were enjoying a sojourn with Bjugstads, church members at First Lutheran and a family with four very musical daughters who lived on a farm off Highway T, just a couple of miles north of the Municipal Airport, and walking distance from home. We might as well have been two thousand miles apart from the girls, since we were out of communication, no telephone numbers having been shared, at least not at the juvenile level.

Darrold, the teenage hired hand, took charge while Mr. and Mrs. A.O. gathered supplies and caught up on gossip in town. Joel, a friend of his whose father sold agricultural machines and raised turkeys on a dense ten-acre plot adjoining A.O.'s south forty, had joined us for the afternoon. Finished with chores, we began preparations. Not that there was a plan. It just fell out. Exploring a section of paving work underway on County Road Double A that ran past A.O.'s driveway, we came upon an important find. Several red danger flags from the construction site furtively tucked underneath t-shirts, we hoofed it up to the gravel driveway. We had set out to collect A.O.'s mail. Road inspection offered a diversion, a reprieve from our appointed task. It turned out to be a double fluke. For in retrieving the newspaper and letters stuffed in A.O.'s mailbox, we solved a huge mystery. One envelope, looking businesslike rather than personal, carried A.O.'s address in full. There it was, all spelled out: A r t h u r   O s c a r   J o h n s o n.

Now we knew!

I remember the sensation of being a participant in a newsworthy world-shaking event, one we could definitely capitalize on. We would set up a booth out in front of our house on the corner of La Salle and Mill. The sign scotch-taped to the card table positioned at the curb would read "Kool-Aid, a Nickle." Small cryptic letters below would add "A.O. X-Planed, a Dime. Don't tell!" We skipped the length of the driveway, celebrating our secret and the prospects for wealth. We were superior creatures. From now on we would be able to buy the things we had to be content only to wish for before—a hunting knife in an embossed leather sheath, a pony, a week at scout camp without having to traipse all over Rice Lake beforehand selling Maxine Soap door-to-door, a packet of mint triangle-shaped, brilliantly colored commemorative stamps from Borneo, Dreamsicles at the Treat Shop every afternoon on the way home from school, a waterproof flashlight with a bracket for mounting on a bike for night rides, as well as dozens of other valuables ogled at in local storefronts or pictured in the Monkey-Ward catalog. And still we would have plenty of money in our presently meager passbook accounts at Barron County National Bank. My twenty-five-dollar U.S. savings bond and the sixty dollars I had accumulated in my paper route bond could remain intact, kept in reserve for the rainy days Mom and Dad and other grown-ups spoke of and worried about. I wouldn't have to go bean picking to get supplies (at Ben Franklin's) and new clothes (at Hanson and Peterson's) for school in the fall. I had become a rich young man. My share in the discovery that day on the farm had put me on the map, at least in Barron County, where my reputation counted the most.

After regaling ourselves with a victory snack of milk and graham crackers back at the house, during which we whispered and munched, savoring our good fortune and imagining ourselves to be pirates with great sacks of loot and chests of rare treasures, we made a beeline for the barn. There we untangled hanks of rope to make bridles for the horses. We flipped coins for the horses and our sequence in the race. Arthur Oscar's draft horses made the ponies we rode at the carnival at the annual Barron Butter Festival seem like animals from the kingdom of Lilliput in *Gulliver's Travels*. Shetland vs. Clydesdale. Out in the barnyard, trudging through the mix of manure, straw, and mud moistened by cattle piss and a recent thundershower, leading our horses by ropes, my mates and I pranced with heroic pride beyond the barbed wire fence to the adjoining grassy pasture, the bucolic scene chosen for our Olympic game. It didn't really matter that spectators had not gathered to witness the competition. I commanded a presence I was later to observe in Dylan Thomas's childhood idyll, "Fern Hill," a poem I related to and read aloud with nostalgic enthusiasm in classrooms ahush with envy and empathy by students afforded a fanciful furlough from their preoccupation with partying and accompanying realities of collegiate life.

Until it came our turn to ride, one of us was held responsible for waving the road flags to signal the start of the race and the other two—independently, for the sake of accuracy and fairness—were to count slowly to see how many seconds it took for the rider to make it from one side of the pasture, past the big elm tree, and back to the open gate leading into the barnyard. There was to be no cheating. None! We placed our right hands on top of one another's while we huddled and pledged to be honest, each to do his best, and all to accept the outcome without a grudge regardless of who won.

It was now my turn to ride. Bareback on my stead, my legs in split position, I hung on to the mane and at the same time, Phil having waved the flags for me to go, clicked and dug my heels into the giant's upper belly. *Gal-uumph. Gal-uumph. Gal-uumph. Gal-uumph.* I started to slip. Still gripping the hair, I slid round the big back and belly and dropped close to the legs in motion. The huge fetlocks a blur as the horse beat the ground. I fell on my back, the horse overhead. Suddenly I knew, not just dreaded, I had joined company with Claus Bergeson.

I only picked beans at Claus Bergeson's once. But it stood as my record: 313 pounds at 2½ cents per pound. It was no easy achievement. I had to keep going, sweaty and thirsty, both hands stained green and too stiff to be of much use the rest of the day. Nowadays workers could sue for damages, specifically for injuries along the lines of carpal tunnel or slipped spinal disc. But I, weary as I was, did not register a complaint. I didn't really get a chance to boast, because everyone weighing in, and later Mom, when I got home, praised me profusely. My pride was well earned. Claus Bergeson's fields were way out and I had to ride an old school bus to get there. I didn't have my bicycle along, so I couldn't peter out when the sun got too hot in the afternoon and head for home or ride to the park and go swimming or, instead—on account of bean-picking season being dog days—play croquet or pitch horseshoes.

Mention of horseshoes brings me precisely to the point! The main reason for people avoiding Claus Bergeson was his face. Disfigured from being kicked by a horse, his head was a fright. One eye slanted and smaller than the other, a nose twisted like modeled clay, and a concavity where a cheek should be to balance both sides, Claus didn't have friends or admirers. We tried to keep from staring, but what could we do? If he were part of a circus freak show, anyone would pay good money, probably a quarter or fifty cents, to catch a look at him. Claus was a poor soul I wouldn't trade places with for any amount of money.

As I sagged over the side of the horse *galumphing* along and approached the ground beneath, I saw in Technicolor the image of Claus Bergeson. In a moment he and I would possess a common fate. I was nearing disaster on what we had naively conceived to be a happy holiday race. It crossed my mind that God was getting even with me for the theft of the road flags. But God evidently had other plans for me than to mimic, for real now, the wretched bean grower. Claus would remain the sole specter of the bean fields. I was to be numbered among the chosen race, those whom we designate as normal. Danger averted me at the last second. Lying on my back I heard the shwoush of hoofs beating and echoing on the earth below. I was not destined to join the disfigured, the lame, or the dead. That day's improvised horse race I neither won nor lost. I came out of it fine.

Later, the only times I got close to draft horses were when we were haying, tractors not yet monopolizing America's Dairyland, watching horse pulling contests at the fair, or seeing Budweiser commercials on TV. I had gotten too close for comfort. My dad had also. One time when we were little, he removed his shirt to reveal the scar he had from being bitten by one such beast on the farm he grew up on outside of Stillwater, Minnesota. It's my belief that while observing harness racing and jockey derbies is much safer and can be great fun, the excitement of participating in a bareback race on draft horses is unmatched for memories. The stay at A.O.'s yielded a twofold triumph: discovery and survival.

≫ • ≪

Paper Routes

One night out collecting on my *Superior Telegram* route, a customer who was three weeks' delinquent in paying threw the money at me—mostly, and deliberately, in pennies. With an angry grunt, as if I had forced the evening papers on her, she flung the cash on the bare floor. Most of the coins rolled under a day bed at one end of the room. I had to slide my arm under and fight dust bunnies for the filthy lucre. Phil and I had observed that with a paper route we had to earn our money twice, once when we delivered the paper and again when we collected. But now, crawling on my hands and knees—literally—to collect the overdue payment, I was earning my money for the third time. Why didn't she pay regularly like good subscribers did? Well, I got even. I quit delivering to her after that incident. I liked it when customers paid each week right on the spot, a few leaving envelopes by the door, so I wouldn't have to knock. When they paid in advance, however, it created accounting difficulties the following weeks when I frantically scrounged for loose change to combine with the coins and wabbed up bills I had in my drawstring bag so I could send off a money order for my weekly paper bill. To this day I don't believe that we actually came out ahead in what had been touted and transferred to us as a profitable, character-building enterprise. As a further

9

motivation of the non-monetary kind, Dad had assured us that a slew of U.S. presidents and famous people had had paper routes and, what's more, had become Eagle scouts.

Because we often subbed for one another, Phil and I had to know each other's route by heart. We'd practice the names in sequence of delivery, sometimes substituting landscape features or other oddities, going through them as fast and faultlessly as we could. The procedure reminded me of when we were called on at Sunday School, Bible School, or Confirmation to recite in order the books of the Bible, from Genesis, Exodus, and Leviticus to Malachai in the Old Testament and clear on through to the Book of Revelation—to add an "s" here was to expose oneself as biblically illiterate—in the New Testament. Thank goodness we weren't Catholics or we'd have had to memorize the Apocrypha to boot. I did envy them the concept of purgatory, though, because it offered a nice safety net for those who couldn't quite make the grade but weren't bad enough to be exiled to hell for keeps.

When they were youngsters, my dad and his brothers and sisters turned the alphabet, one of the first things kids commit to memory, into a pronounceable polysyllabic word: Abkedefaghijikalowmunopquristu-vawxyz, or something close to that. Challenging our memories, we'd march through the states, naming the capital cities, in a broad sweep from the Atlantic to the Pacific. One of our puzzles when put together made up a map of the states. Because it had all the capitals printed on it, we quickly mastered that aspect of geography. Hardest of all was listing the American presidents in chronological order. At school we had to memorize the multiplication tables and be able to count by twos, threes, whatever, as far as we could go. It all was good exercise if a bit taxing sometimes. We were taught never to consider any knowledge as trivia, and those were the days when students were expected to memorize things. We had to know by heart long passages from Shakespeare, the Bible, Luther's *Small Catecism*, and other significant documents, like Lincoln's Gettysburg Address and a good portion of the Declaration of Independence. In high school, teachers encouraged their prize students to rehearse and recite declamations, lengthy formal essays imbued with great emotional and rhetorical appeal. Memorization was in!

Anyway, it was supremely important to keep track of customers on the route. Else after supper I was apt to hear Mom on the telephone. "Yes, I'm sure he just forgot. He did mention that he had an extra paper left over tonight. He'll be right over with it." Then instead of just folding the thing into thirds so the tucked paper could be thrown from my bike up onto the porch, I'd have to park my bike, putting the kickstand down firmly on the sidewalk, and walk up to the house, ring the bell or knock on the door, face the inconvenienced customer, and hand him the paper, muttering a stock apology. If I listened close, I might hear a gratuitous but sympathetic "I'm sorry" issue from the Mrs. back in the kitchen. Immediately the transaction was over, I tore away, first vowing never to return to the scene but then modifying the vow to never missing their paper again.

I felt blessed when customers lived in consecutive houses or weren't too far apart. Just by experimenting with different ways to connect my stops and configure my route, I could cut down the time and distance required to complete it by seconds if not minutes. It helped if I could solicit new customers to fill in the spaces and replace those that quit. Contests were offered to get new customers. The lure would be prizes per number of new customers gained. Phil got to attend the Winter Carnival in St. Paul because he succeeded in tallying twenty new customers during a two-week effort to expand subscribers. That was with the *St. Paul Pioneer Press*. The *Superior Evening Telegram* was stingier. More people were interested in happenings in the Twin Cities than in Superior and Duluth. This fact was borne out by the size of the gaps between my customers, which made for a pretty long route. Fortunately, however, the *Telegram* didn't put out a Sunday paper. Come Saturday I always had a day off.

But on the Sabbath I helped Phil do his morning route. We made sure we got up early to make it down to the old fire department garage where the papers were spilled out in bundles by a guy who trucked them there from the Cities in the middle of the night. Delivering Sunday papers in winter was no picnic. Phil and I would head out before dawn, bundled up in our parkas, scarves over our mouths, feet double socked and galoshes buckled, mittens protected by leather chockers. We trudged along, crunching the new-fallen snow beneath our feet, pulling the sled behind us, our breaths lingering like lazy smoke in front of our frosted faces. Nobody and nothing stirred. After the first ten deliveries, we'd stop at a coffee shop that opened early for breakfast to get coffee and doughnuts before returning to the paper shed for a fresh supply of newspapers. Two bundles later, another hour's exposure to sub-zero temperatures, we'd stop at the Creamery to warm up again. Pulling papers on the sled, going back to the old fire department shed for more, pliers in hand to cut the wire binding the bundles, no more than twenty per bunch, so thick the Sunday edition, taking a couple of breaks from the cold, getting all seventy or eighty papers properly accounted for. It was a grueling test of our stamina for survival. But besides keeping us in pocket change, delivering Sunday papers in wintertime built memories and, presumably, character at the same time.

The *Telegram* came into Barron on the train and we picked up our supply at the Depot. They were generally thinner—not that much going on in Northern Wisconsin—so the bag, carried over our shoulder on days we walked the route, flung into our basket when we biked, didn't bulge as much as it would if it had been the *Pioneer Press* or the *Minneapolis Star and Tribune*. The big city papers, riddled with stories of unspeakable yet printable crimes, were so bulky, especially on Sundays, but swollen as well on Wednesdays, that we had to make several trips back and forth to get all our newspapers distributed. We had it down so pat that occasionally we'd even find ourselves going through this routine in the blurry version of a dream.

ဢ • ဢ

The Yellow River

On the west side of Barron the Yellow River forms a small lake above the dam and power plant. Across the lake to the north stands a ramshackle barn, the roof sagging, the windows all broken. As with other dilapidated structures—the place we claimed was haunted, a ruined house (with tattered wallpaper and stacks of unread old newspapers) aslant on the horizon like an unglorified Tower of Pisa, only a mile from Sandy Cliff, where we loved to cook out and camp; the rotten fence posts and crumbling gate (or stile) that marked the holdings of a ne'er-do-well farmer, an incongruity in Barron County; waterlogged boats long ago abandoned by their owners and, therefore, deemed public property by lads out for adventure—the old icehouse asked to be taken over. We were always on the alert for such opportunities.

Just below the dam, over in waters less roily than what came thundering over the dam, we fished for bullheads. Daredevils, worms, insects—bullheads were suckers for any bait. They always put up a great fight. They weren't much for nibbling; they preferred a gluttonous grab. Therefore, it was usually a decisive strike. Once hoisted out of the water, they continued the battle, flopping any which way, cutting us with their gills and searing us with their horns. They wouldn't yield. Even while stripping them clean of their slimy skin with a pliers we often got stung and bled. If we could have afforded it or had it to do over again, we'd have brought them in with nets and put on gloves to carry them home where we could use the big vise on Dad's workbench to hold them still while we peeled them alive. Frankly, they weren't all that good eating. Nothing like northerns. With bullheads we were in it for the sport alone.

To the east, across the bridge where a county road passed by the golf course and wended its way out to farms, the river became part of the park. It was here that Barronites picnicked, played baseball and tennis, and went swimming. (If we had a church group we could reserve the pavilion and dominate the park that afternoon, dishing out gobs of fried chicken, potato salad, baked beans, Jell-O, and Dixie Cups for dessert.) Beyond the spillway a hundred yards further east, the river was joined by the branch diverting from the power plant, over which an arched wooden bridge painted marine green—the same green applied to the posts bordering the park—and supported by cables underneath, gave access to the bathhouse and swimming area on one side and the pavilion and ball diamond on the other. On this side of the spillway two ropes with bobbers streched the width of the cement-walled section of river enclosing the swimming area.

The ropes demarcated the three parts. The first, being the shallowest and distinguished by the sloped concrete apron provided for entry, was designated the Little Part. It was reserved for beginners. The Middle Part was restricted to those who had passed the test qualifying them as intermediates, a rigorous two laps of keeping afloat by holding onto a swim board and kicking up a storm. The third section, which incorporated a diving platform on the south side and the spillway on the east side, was the deep end, aptly named the Big Part. For advanced swimmers, those who had proven their prowess by swimming twice the length of the three parts using the Australian crawl stroke plus negotiating an extra half length underwater, the Big Part offered the novelty of crossing the river by way of the spillway. Our feet, toes cramped up for safety and spread out from the force, would feel the invigorating, strong flow of the river as gravity sucked the eager water over the two-foot wide dam, beneath which it tumbled and roared before rushing onward.

The diving platform had two boards, a high and a low. A person on the upper level had priority. The low board jutted out about three feet above the water's surface and was two of so feet shorter. The difference in length was to prevent accidents should divers neglect to observe protocol. To cannon ball from the high dive was a thrill discouraged by the lifeguards, who every once in a while dove fancy dives to show off and set an example of what exactly was tolerated in the way of maritime gymnastics at the City Park. But after hours we could do anything. And we did everything!

In the Big Part we trained for and completed the Red Cross Life Saving Certificate as well as the requirements for Swimming Merit Badge. On the day our final session of life saving was scheduled, Dick Kirkwood, Gene Knowlton, and Phil, and I rode our bikes—a Schwinn, a Hawthorne, a Monarch, and one an unidentifiable brand—from Barron on Highway 8 all the way to Saint Croix Falls, Minnesota, and back home, an exhausting one-hundred-mile journey contending with vast hills and busy traffic. Critics might dismiss the event as a mere biathalon but we waxed heroic from the ordeal, especially when the *News-Shield* featured an article about us in the next week's issue. How we got our jeans off in the water, managed to tie the pant legs together and blow them full of air, our lungs having endured a colossal workout before entering the water, is hard even now to believe. The pants got puffed up, we rescued our pretend drowning victims, and, consequently, we passed the final test that night before turning in.

Christie, one of the twins, was a little fish. Darting about the water like a minnow, "Christie," Mom exclaimed, "is really a mermaid in disguise—right out of Hans Christian Andersen." She graduated to the Big Part when others her age were still enjoying the thrill of splashing in the wading pool back of the bathhouse. All five of us children, three girls and two boys, were quick to inherit the Big Part. We got strong parental encouragement. Our family took frequent car trips to visit swimming beaches in outlying towns. The sequence was swim and then picnic. Home of the Rutabaga Festival, Cumberland, ten miles to the northeast on Highway 25, had been settled by Italians. The town's claim to fame was a restaurant with the world's best spaghetti. Cumberland also boasted a bathing area with the tallest slide around. In Rice Lake, a town sited on the shore of its namesake lake, even our dog, Domino, joined in the bathing spree, first testing his dog paddle stroke in a fountain that was the centerpiece for the park-cum-swimming beach. Haywood, Spooner, Shell Lake, Turtle Lake, Amery, Cameron, Chetek, Ladysmith, Poskin—every town around had swimming accommodations, though none rivaled those of the Barron Park. That fact can easily be verified by asking any resident or the numerous visitors the park drew from far and wide.

Alas! No longer do Barronites swim in the Yellow River. A tapwater fed and cholorine-laced pool now provides them delight in the summer. Because they don't have the experience and memories we have of yore, however, it must seem to them to be unmatched anytime anyplace.

In our time, guys contested to see who would jump in earliest each season. We had to brace ourselves and just go for it. I don't think I exactly set the record, but I do recall taking a dip on my birthday, April 28th, one year. The top layer was cold, all right, yet only as I sank deeper could I appreciate the fact that the river had thawed but a few weeks before. God, who controls nature's thermostat and sets the calendar of seasons, had obviously not yet beckoned the sun to usher in summer's heat.

During flood days in early summer, the spillway looked like a bulge in the river. The speed of the current was wonderful as we floated along over the water lilies, either as human buoys or, more cautiously, on inner tubes patched and judged seaworthy for the voyage. Where the branch converged with the major waterway coming from the spillway, the current increased to the point parents would regard as alarming. "That's not safe," they would pontificate, without any experience or actual proof, as we peered out the car window at the unruly river at flood stage. That's of course why the city would post a temporary sign: "DANGER. FLOODING."

It never precisely said "SWIMMING NOT ALLOWED," I think because nobody thought boys would be so daring or so foolish.

Elsewhere along the river and throughout the countryside we rarely came across "NO TRESPASSING" signs. Even above the dam. Naturally, we felt at liberty to cross the cabled-together logs floating near the dam where they were to serve to block large debris from cascading over. Phil and I and cousin Bob Substad, who lived in Minneapolis where he was active in YMCA and shared Diamond Lake and Minnehaha Falls and traffic with a big-city population, paddled our new boat across the lake to the old icehouse an afternoon in late July. We had just finished the last phase of its construction and the paint was good and dry. The tumble-down barn translated into an island fort that had to withstand the attack we pirates were bent on carrying out now that we had landed. When we had beat our way into the structure, killed all the enemies, and taken charge with appropriate gestures and verbiage, we climbed to the top of the sawdust stack to survey the kingdom that was now ours. Rather than rest on our laurels or our behinds we continued our exploits. We explored the premises on hands and knees and then dug down to see what was beneath the sawdust and shavings. Dull brown on the exterior, the wood chips became brighter and redder the further we excavated. Then a discovery! Big blocks of ice, cold as when they had been cut and hauled from the frozen river in January. What fun to lick ice in the middle of summer. It beat all popsicles, regardless of flavor. From root beer to cherry to grape, orange, and strawberry, we had tasted them all. Rubbing our tongues over the frigid clear glass crystal cubes that summer afternoon, quenching our thirst as no popsicle, glass of lemonade, or bottle of Squirt ever could, threw us back to times in the winter spent rollicking in snowbanks and licking icicles ripped from the eaves where they hung like stalactites remembered from family excursions to Crystal Cave. Water is fascinating the way it changes its state according to the temperature. Water is a world of wonder for a child. That day we were inspired by ice!

∽ • ଓ

Down the Hayshoot

Having grown up in rural Wisconsin, in a county famous for its dairy farms, I became acquainted with the perils of farm life at an early age. I don't simply have in mind failed crops, snow-bound stretches in the winter, wall-to-wall chores, tractor mishaps, or any other of the myriad accident-prone, comfort-stingy features associated with existence on a farm.

In junior high I won an award from the REA for my essay on the topic Rural Lifestyle Prior to Electrification. Pretty good for a boy who wasn't FFA, took Shop instead of Ag, joined Boy Scouts not 4-H, didn't have experience showing a calf or garden produce at the fair, and lived in town! Well, Barron was itself an introduction to farm life. Two blocks west and there was the Olsens' farm. A hike or short bike ride in any direction got us into woods and pastures, haymows and silos, creeks and cornfields. I gained firsthand experience in farming by dint of being friends and schoolmates with kids from farms. Occasionally I would ride the bus home from school with country kids. I'd help with milking, stripping the teats after the milking machines had drawn their quota, wave my hand through the chilled water in the milk house, adjust the bails as the combine spit them up to the hay rack, shovel out and lime down the barn gutters, and fill the troughs and check the water levers at each stanchion. Akin to veteran farmers, I spouted my preferences on such matters as Holsteins vs. Guernseys, Rhode Island Reds vs. Leghorns, alfalfa vs. timothy and clover, Allis Chalmer vs. Farmall, Massey Ferguson, John Deere, or Ford. Believe me, that wasn't lore derived over the years from time spent wandering around Machinery Hill and the livestock and produce barns at the Minnesota State Fair. Indeed, our family harvested sweet corn and tomatoes in the backyard and raised chickens and collected our own eggs right in town.

It was a life at one with nature. Adjoining our double lot was Thompson's Woods, two acres of wilderness providing Phil and me and our gang opportunity for building tree houses and swinging Tarzan fashion on vines from tree to tree. During long hot humid summers the Yellow River and Quaderer's Creek filled in the blanks with bouts of

frog catching, fishing, swimming, and boating. Winters weren't just for shoveling and shivering. That was the season dedicated to skating on neighborhood rinks and nearby rivers, sledding on Bull Hill, skiing down surrounding slopes and across the golf course, and tobogganing at breakneck speed on Dragseths' farm January afternoons after emptying plates of fried chicken, mixed vegetables (with too many peas and carrots and not enough corn), mashed potatoes, and apple pie al a mode. Country and town, summer and winter—two grand hemispheres of a single whole world.

But, as I was noting, farm life was not easy. Risks and dangers lurked even in Paradise. Thrilling it was to be out in the air enjoying the sight of blue sky and puffy clouds overhead when busy threshing. Though the sweat was chronic and the flies were thick, the smell of silage was tonic to the lungs of a city boy. So too the tang of freshly mowed hay. To sit aboard a manure spreader or take turns riding the barn cleaning trolley oblivious to odors! That was a condition peculiar to childhood.

One day I got to experience the adulthood side of farming while cavorting about the hayloft. Happy in my realm above, while whistling and musing, I all of a sudden lost my footing when I stepped unawares into a hayshoot. Down I shot into the underworld, nine feet below, into a cattle pen whose concrete floor was layered with straw.

In the split second of my fall a single thought ripped through my brain. It wasn't the conviction that I would be dead upon arrival but the certainty that I would be maimed for life. Life imprisonment instead of the electric chair. An image of Mr. Wolf arose in utter clarity. I was sure that my head would be lodged in my shoulders, my neck gone, broken, and I would pass for a young version of poor old Mr. Wolf. Countless times walking or biking down to the park I passed Mr. Wolf out mowing his grass. All those sights now coalesced into one haunting picture, which came instantly to mind while I descended. An ancient manual mower serving as a prop, the dejected figure stretched his head and eyes upward trying to catch a level look at the lawn ahead. Whenever and wherever he went beyond the premises, Mr. Wolf would be seen walking in the same manner, chin to his chest, back arched, struggling in vain to catch a view more expansive than that of the lower regions for which he would have to settle. "There but by the grace of God go we," we would mutter to ourselves when we encountered Mr. Wolf on his arduous perambulations about town. Now I would share his fate. The fall—really, my landing from the fall—would cause an abrupt shock to my frame. My head would no longer provide the easy full view I had enjoyed of my universe. It would hang against my chest and I would have to work like hell to see anything in front of me. Miraculously, I survived the fall intact, just a bit out of breath, my only witness a stupefied heifer. Mr. Wolf would have to go it alone.

After that incident in the barn, I became more aware of the potential for danger that existed in rural America. I had come of age. It was a rite of initiation. I stepped more gingerly thereafter, whether while playing cowboy in the hayloft or upon entering the sandpit where we swam illegally on sunny afternoons and starlit evenings. The lesson that carried over into adulthood was that you must ever be on guard. What we learned in Boy Scouts about being prepared somehow had not transferred into reality until that fall from hay to straw.

From Jack Sprat's to the Treat Shop: A Walk through Town

Jack Sprat's, a small grocery store run by Harvey Paulson, stood conveniently on a corner of La Salle Avenue, the main street in Barron, two blocks east of our house. The store was a converted house and, therefore, unintentionally, continued to contribute to the residential character of the neighborhood. Jack Sprat's was handy to Ward School when we took that way going home, so it was a regular source for candy bars, Cracker Jacks, and popsicles when we had the nickels to buy them. For a while we had been able to charge them, but Mom and Dad put a stop to that when the bills mounted and payments weren't keeping even with charges.

When Mr. Paulson got down a box of cereal we asked for, he'd use a stick that had a metal hoop on one end to fetch it from one of the high shelves. He was good at catching items. When we bought lunch-meat, he'd run it through a hand-cranked stainless steel cutter, slicing it thick unless we specifically asked for thin slices. We got to sample before deciding what kind, but bologna was the cheapest and, therefore, the question was moot. Slapping the slices on to a piece of waxed paper, he'd weigh the stack on a shiny white scale that showed the customer the number of ounces and pounds through a magnifying lens that faced both ways. With his left hand he'd reach up and grab the end of the string that hung down from the spool above, which unwound from a little doweled sconce to thread its way round a small pulley and through an eyelet connected to a spring mechanism. With three wraps around his left palm, the end of the string held tightly between his pinkie and the rest of his fingers, he'd twist it around the parcel, deftly tying it with a secure but easily removed slip knot. Meanwhile, with his free right hand he'd rip off a generous length of stiff white paper from a roll snugged tight by a bar with a serrated edge and fold it to form a flat packet that resembled a man's large handkerchief starched and creased to look fancy. "Anything else today?" he'd ask before selecting an appropriately sized brown paper sack in which to place the packet along with the loaf of bread and the "anything else" on our list. As we left we couldn't help gazing longingly at the comic books on the rack by the door: "Archie," "Superman," "Popeye," "Little Audrey"—they all looked intriguing and sold at a dime apiece. We'd pass them up and satisfy ourselves with the knowledge that we could trade comics this week with Charles Ness or some other friend we hadn't recently exchanged with.

The landmark downtown Barron was the large stone courthouse occupying an entire block on the south side of La Salle. It was set back

on a hill, which made it look more important and at the same time allowed for seating on the lawn that ran down to a cement wall framing the sidewalk below. It was here that a big granite stone gave information about John Quaderer, a local hero remembered for having stolen back from Rice Lake the document, dated 1870 something, designating Barron as the location for the county seat. And it was here, on the grassy eminence, that people gathered to watch parades and enjoy the afternoon talent show and nightly programs presented on a platform temporarily erected on the blocked-off street during the Barron Butter Festival held in late July or early August.

On that same side of La Salle and just west of the courthouse visitors could find lodging at the Stewart Hotel. It had become primarily an apartment complex of late but its façade and large porch still gave a prestigious look. A Shell Oil station commanded the corner site to the east. The structures edging the rest of that side of the street, heading on east, included a dry cleaner's, a tavern, an insurance agency, and, on the next corner, one of the two banks in town. The Farmer's Store (an old-fashioned general or department store with a ceiling three stories high, balconies and a grand wooden staircase supplementing the merchandise space on the main floor and in the basement, and a vacuum tube system that sucked containers with cash and receipts back and forth between levels) competed with Snyder's Grocery next door.

Occupying the next block east, behind which was the Barron Cooperative Creamery, its chimneys always emitting hot vapors, was the high school, which by a special arrangement was heated by surplus steam piped over to radiators from the Creamery. A three-story brick building, the high school enclosed a gymnasium (slash) auditorium, classrooms, band and choral practice rooms, teachers' offices and lounge, a pair of girls' and boys' lavatories, separate shops for industrial arts and "ag," and a lunchroom and adjoining kitchen.

A large study hall dominated the third floor. It served collaterally as a library, one side of the hall covered with shelving containing books considered fit reading and reference material for small-town teenagers. In the study hall we were supposed to keep quiet. Teachers took turns monitoring from the desk at the front. But students disobediently chewed gum, threw spit wads, passed notes, and whispered as if it were a free-for-all. One afternoon after lunch hour, the principal, Mr. Hoare, who was on guard then, was accosted by a student who had the reputation of being a hoodlum. The verbal exchange became louder and turned vulgar. Then the student let loose with his fist. The altercation ended quickly—too soon to suit many of the spectators—when Mr. Hoare, a sturdy man who didn't brook rebellion, got the kid in a hammerlock and marched him down to his office, where he was officially suspended, that is, deprived of school privileges for the remainder of the school year. Mr. Hoare had had trouble before with the kid and knew it would be counterproductive to expel him and futile to slap him with more detention hours. The main thing was to subdue and humiliate him in front of the audience he had attracted with his blackboard jungle behavior.

Leaving the school and the topic of decorum behind, as we traveled eastward on La Salle, we'd see houses and nothing commercial till we reached the outskirts. Where the street curved to join Highway 8 (which through town was street-signed Division Avenue), we hit a bridge. It was the other end of the Yellow River, which at this end too spread out to form a pond. A smaller dam to the right of the bridge once powered the old Munsingwear plant, now abandoned and good only for the stone and mortar abutments which provided a platform to fish from. A hundred yards farther, set back from the road, sat the new REA headquarters, and smack dab at the fork of La Salle and Division, we were hailed by the East End Market. Ahead were three other signs. The one on the north side, a companion to the signs located at the other three entries to Barron, marked the city limits and recorded the population, the other two signs respectively governing the speeds of vehicles coming and going. From then on farmland and woods wherever we looked. If we kept going in that direction on Highway 8 in a car moving along at fifty-five miles per hour, we'd arrive in Cameron in six or seven minutes. From Cameron the most immediate options were threefold: Rice Lake, Ladysmith, or Chetek.

If we were to double back and head west from the high school, the two buildings to note on the block opposite, each commanding a corner, were the Barron Rest Home and the Treat Shop. The rest home was a must among stops made by Luther Leaguers and other holiday groups out caroling. The old men sitting around in long underwear and the old ladies bundled up in bathrobes or with cardigans pulled snugly over their dresses and wearing heavy hosiery, few of them with any teeth left to chew, woke up from their naps and put aside their aimless chattering to listen. Their sobs and sighs and blowing of noses accompanied the singing. On school days on the next corner students milled outside the Treat Shop. Those that were still inside trying to decide among sweets were aided in their choice by the proprietors, DPs who gave excited advice in fluent German. *"Yah, das ist sehr gut und nur funf fennies!"*

A jaunt westward along the sunny side of La Salle Avenue took us past Chirhart's Chevrolet dealership, Gamble's, Eulen's Jewelry, Helmer Wiegen's Clover Farm Store, out in front of which during yuletide tubs crammed full of lutefisk soaking in cold lye water got our attention, the Pal Café, a popular hangout after basketball games, a trio of professional offices housing a lawyer, a dentist, and a doctor, and, most fun, the Majestic theatre. Several staples—Ben Franklin's Five and Ten, Morrison's Pharmacy, the Coast-to-Coast hardware store, where my brother got caught shoplifting a doodad for his bike and had to go back with Dad and vow never to do so again, Erickson's Grocery, where we did our major shopping, Hanson and Peterson's Clothing, my bank, a bakery, and the post office—took charge of the block fronting the court house. At the other corner of the block before Jack Sprat's was Stebbins' Drug Store. Go by the *News-Shield* and two houses and we could spot Harvey Paulson through the window of the door leading into his store.

This was the day of the soda fountain and soda jerk. We quaffed a good many lime phosphates and cherry and chocolate Cokes and licked numerous single and double-dipped ice cream cones of all flavors in those years, especially at Stebbins'. At Stebbins', Phil and I also bought bottles of denatured alcohol and other supplies to fuel Bunsen burners and conduct chemistry experiments in our basement.

On the side streets and strung out along Division Avenue sundry other establishments flourished, among them a couple of auto repair garages, including Richie's, where we could always hit them up for a free inner tube, all decorated with red-and-black patches bearing the legacy of a string of little misfortunes that popped up along the road of life; a pool hall, said to be incredibly smoky and noisy; Punky Samuel's Bar; an appliance store; a furniture and carpet store; a welding and machine shop; the fire station; the police station; two funeral parlors; offices of other doctors, a second dentist, veterinarians, and more attorneys; eight or nine churches; Ward Elementary School; the depot; a stockyard and auction barn; a lumber company; an auto body shop; the Ford-Mercury-Edsel-and-Lincoln dealership; a drive-in A &W root beer stand; a Dairy Queen; the elevator, where farmers could deliver grain and buy gunny sacks of feed and seed; a tractor and farm implement business; and a family-type restaurant.

On the street leading to the west entry to the park, less than a block from where Toby Thompson lived, the Carnegie Library and the Legionnaires' log cabin took up prominent space. The Legionnaires' was where our Scout meetings, Troop #6, were held. We snubbed Troop #73, which met in the basement of the Methodist Church, except when we shared foreign ground for a Skill-o-ree or faced each other at Camp Phillips for a week of nearly solid cookouts and contests to see which patrols could lash together a bridge or a lookout tower the fastest, using the proper knots and depending only on saplings and fallen branches nearby. The Flying Eagle, the patrol my brother and I and closest friends were members of, rotated its meeting among the houses of the members' families. Pancake suppers, put on as fund raisers for our troop to replenish supplies our quartermaster reported as "insufficient to keep the ball rolling," which made it sound like we were a bowling team and members of an amateur league, brought many townsfolk to the cabin and required our collective salesmanship to get all the tickets sold. It was an eat-all-you-can affair, and we got to stuff ourselves free when everyone had departed for their couches back home.

The library was a gold mine, and we were the prospectors. During the summer it was a race to see who could read and report on the most books. I dug into the explorer series with titles like *Daniel Boone*, *Davy Crockett*, and *Lewis and Clark*. A biography of the Wright Brothers inspired my brother and me and Dick Kirkwood to set up a bicycle repair business. After a couple of requests for our services and too much time and money spent building up an inventory of parts, we gave it up. Later, upon building our first and only boat, that selfsame entrepreneurial spirit prompted us to draw plans for a boat-making shop, another pipe dream. The deal at the library was that we got a colored circle for each book we read and reported on. The circles had the titles printed on them and, when posted on the wall next to our names, formed bookworms. The longer the worm the greater the chance you'd win one of the top three prizes at the close of the summer. We could increase our own personal library that way. It helped too to have an uncle who owned a book store. Uncle Art in New York sent all of us children books on our birthdays and at Christmas. In our household reading was more entrenched even than listening to the radio or the phonograph or, when we finally got a set, watching television.

Over the years in Barron we explored every surface, practically every cubic inch, of every building. We took possession. Later, when we moved away, I felt that I had sold my birthright or abandoned the ship like a sea captain in a storm. With Toby and a band of other friends, on the eve before the moving van came to our house, I felt pangs of nostalgia and shivers of excitement simultaneously while we talked for the last time and listened to "It's Almost Tomorrow" on the jukebox at the Pal Café. I was fifteen years old and knew I was at a crossroads and life would never be the same. Yes, I would visit again, even returning to work at Badger Turkey Industries and live with Toby for the summer between graduating from Sioux City Central and matriculating at St. Olaf, a church-related liberal arts college in Northfield, Minnesota. But as the wise man observed and many of us have experience to prove, we can't really go home again once we've left.

The Majestic

M ovies, consisting of moving pictures actually projected in the-
atres and shown on large indoor or outdoor screens, served
as a bridge spanning radio and television. Their uniqueness
resided in their being community events. As in a theatre production or
a symphony orchestra concert, a true sense of audience is present in listening to a radio delivered program. With a movie at a show hall, before
lights dim and curtains open and afterwards when the procedure is
reversed and movie-goers are exiting, the people attending the show
notice others and are aware of being participants in a group experience.
Not so when viewing a video alone, not quite so with close friends or
family watching either.

The drive-in outdoor movie theatre in Rice Lake was a big hit
for nearly two decades. On Buck Night, families, couples, and groups of
friends streamed in for double features. During intermission especially,
but all night long, the concession stand hopped with sales of buttered
popcorn and pop as individuals, twosomes, threesomes, and gangs of
people spilled out of vehicles and crowded in to purchase treats and use
the restrooms. When it wasn't Buck Night, guys might make it a bargain
anyway by driving in and unloading two passengers from the trunk

moments after they got situated and had attached the speaker to the car window. Another version was to let a few guys off on a back road which they could follow and enter from in the rear by climbing over the fence once it was dark enough to pull off the deed. Once in, they'd split off in different directions and each casually stroll toward the concession stand as if they had come from separate vehicles. When they had used the facilities, gone to the toilet and sipped from the water fountain, they would return to their temporarily vacated seats in a convincingly nonchalant fashion, literally taking their ill-gotten treat in stride.

In the little town of Cameron, maybe a quarter the size of Barron and a dwarf by comparison with a giant like Rice Lake, citizens took things entirely into their own hands. They'd sponsor a series in which three or four black-and-white vintage movies would be shown for free in the park over the summer months. The projector was rigged up in the bed of a pickup, plywood painted white and lag-screwed for the season to a couple of permanently planted telephone poles served for a screen, and people sat on blankets, camp stools, or folding chairs and brought their own refreshments. It was paid for by donations. One could, but

didn't have to, give a dollar or change to the aproned neighbor who stood at the park's entrance to direct traffic to the parking area. In addition, right before the show began, local business establishments were publicly thanked by the mayor for their generous sponsorship. Their support was also recognized in newspaper announcements of the upcoming free show.

In Barron and across the country during the middle '40s and '50s Westerns were all the rage. Bigger than life and as real as life, Roy Rogers and Trigger, his horse, and Dale, his wife, and Gabby Hayes, their fat old friend, rode on the silver screen. Friday night's repertoire of cowboys and Indians at the Majestic Theatre included Tom Mix, the Lone Ranger, Hopalong Cassidy—to name a few. Stuart Davis had a going concern at the Majestic. Movies were shown all week, two performances per night, double features, matinees on Saturday and Sunday afternoons, serials and newsreels, advertisements, and previews—cartoons thrown in as a bonus. The Majestic outdid the business that went to the barber shop, which sat right next to it. Only two chairs and one haircut at a time in the old barber shop whereas a show could fill the house, as it often did. And it didn't take *Ben Hur* to do it. Westerns on Friday and Saturday nights played to a packed theatre. Everyone liked movies.

"Everybody Will Be There"

It was suppertime, and the entire family was seated around the table eating when I said, loud enough for Dad to hear, "Phil, Dick told me at school yesterday he's going to the show tonight. Roy Rogers is in it, and everybody's going."

"Yah! I'd like to go too," my brother replied. Dad, however, continued to eat his potatoes as if nothing had been said. The hint had failed.

After supper Phil and I carried the dirty dishes from the dining room into the kitchen—our usual post-meal chore—while Carole and the twins, Christie and Connie, adjourned to the kitchen to wash the dishes, their customary job. Our task completed, we invited Mom into the den to relax with us. She consented. I knew by the perceiving smile on her face that she already suspected a conspiracy in the works. When the three of us were seated on the sofa, we all began to talk at once, although Phil and I ceased when we heard Mom saying, "You fellows want to go to the show, don't you?"

"Yah!" Phil, who was a year older than I, chimed in.

"Everybody will be there. Can we go, Mom?" I begged.

"Well, I'll bring Father a cup of coffee. When he gets into a pleasant mood, you boys tell him what you told me," Mom instructed us, as she always did when we asked to go to a show. Then Mom left the room to carry out her mission.

Phil and I were talking when Mom returned. "Dad's in the study now," she interrupted. "It's nearly six o'clock. You'd better speak to him before it gets too late."

The conspiracy had been formed. Now was the proper time for the attack.

We hurriedly approached Father's study. Boldly, Phil knocked once on his door.

"Come in!" he roared. We pushed open the heavy oak door and stepped quietly into the room.

"Dad, may we go to the show tonight?" Phil pleaded in as humble a tone as he could. We had discovered from previous experience that humility affected Dad's discretion to our favor.

Father began as we could have predicted from times before when we made the same pitch. "Oh!" he protested. "Haven't you boys already seen one show this week? I haven't the money anyway."

"No, Dad," Phil retaliated, "we haven't been to a movie since last Saturday."

Noticing that Phil had gained courage and a little ground, I added, "Everybody is going to be there tonight."

Father weakened. "Well, what's showing?" he muttered.

"Roy Rogers is in it," I stammered.

"Yah!" Phil exclaimed, "It's *Springtime in the Rockies*."

"Go ask your mother," he told us. Dad always sent us to Mom when we had him nearly convinced we should be allowed to go. Consequently, in the interest of speeding up the procedure, we had learned to ask Mom first. We informed him that Mom was all for the idea. At this point, however, Dad must have questioned our integrity. He strode out of the study in pursuit of Mother. We followed. Finding her in the kitchen putting the clean dry dishes back in the cupboard, he asked, as if looking for an ally in a battle about to be lost, "Margaret, do you think the boys should go to a show tonight?"

"Oh, Van," she responded, "this isn't a school night, and they would like very much to see this picture."

"Oh, all right! I'll drive down to the theater to see what type of picture it is," Dad announced. And he left us standing there still in suspense. As long as I can recall going to shows, I remember Dad insisting on seeing the billboard illustration of the movie before giving his sanction. If there appeared to be too much "worldliness" portrayed, that is, excessive shooting and undue sex appeal, we either were barred from that particular movie or had a more difficult time persuading him to let us go. In an amount of time that seemed to us comparable to the duration of the Flood, Dad returned from his errand. Fortunately, the commercial artists of Hollywood had chosen to depict the theme of this motion picture in an unworldly fashion, for Dad informed us, more sternly than cheerfully, "You may go if you have the money."

The first and major battle—getting Dad's permission to attend the show—had been won. Now we were confronted with the problem of locating sufficient monetary means, the atrocious fee of twelve cents each, to turn our dream into reality. Occasionally, Dad shelled out the necessary amount, but he did not offer this time. We were of course always open for donations first. Next, we considered loans. Our final resource involved the confiscation of our own treasures. Mother donated fifteen cents to the cause, but we were still nine cents short. Then Phil and I went upstairs to dig up some rare item that would arouse the buying spirit in the girls. Phil

searched the closet shelves while I ransacked the junk-drawer in our sec-
ond-hand bureau. I cast aside a giant steely and a worn-out fountain pen
to get my hand on "the article of the evening"—a little dime bank that was
a replica of a store cash register. Phil too was buoyed up by the prospect
of selling the bank to one of our bidding sisters. We summoned the girls,
who came into our room directly. Realizing that this was an auction, they
took their places intent on purchasing a suitable item at a bargain rate.
Their behavior became similar to that of mothers in a department store on
the last shopping day before Christmas. Connie, a thrifty brunette who
from time to time surprised us by having managed to accumulate a small
fortune, after having bid several times on her first bid, bought the empty
bank for eleven cents. We could generally count on an auction to balloon
our funds by a dime or more. Since we had exceeded our goal by two
cents, Phil suggested, "Let's get eight cents more somewhere, so we'll each
have a nickel to spend." In such an emergency, Mom would usually come
up with a job for us to do, for which she would pay us the desired amount
Tonight, however, time was limited.

Realizing we didn't have time to earn the difference or for Mom
to make popcorn for us to bring along, I lit on what was our last resort.
"Phil, let's go to the coin collection!"

"Well, Danny, I s'pose we better," he said hesitatingly. The coin
collection Aunt Bert had helped us get started included Indianhead pennies, V nickels, and a variety of less rare specimens. After briefly discussing options, we agreed to rob the collection of a Liberty nickel minted in 1941 and three fairly recent Lincoln pennies. We wouldn't really
miss them, we rationalized.

The procurement of funds to attend the movies proved interesting and required much ingenuity. Nevertheless, during those years, I
always felt that if Dad would have given us each an allowance, our pre-
show frustration would have been greatly alleviated. Phil and I never had
the audacity to suggest such a thing to Dad, though.

Having gathered the luxurious sum of thirty-four cents, we tore
downstairs to put on our winter apparel. Mother heard us and came to

assist. She buckled our rubber boots, zipped up our jackets, handed us our ear muffs, and secured scarves around our faces. "Be careful, keep warm, and have fun," Mom yelled to us as we spilled out the front door. We were off to the show. The twins were young and weren't yet affected by the spirit of the show. They were content to spend Saturday evenings absorbed in coloring books or cutting out paper dolls. Carole, who was a year younger than I but two years older than the twins, was permitted one movie per month. Fortunately, it wasn't her turn tonight. We had enough problems to contend with.

Snow was gently falling, and there was no trace of a wind. Even the sharpness of the sub-zero temperature was greatly reduced by our face scarves. We walked along, chattering and laughing. Phil and I always ran every other block, only stopping to toss snowballs at street-light poles. (At greater distances, Phil was more accurate than I. He was ahead of me in a lot of things, being a year older.)

Before we became aware of the coldness of the December night, we arrived in front of the theatre, stamping our feet to knock off the packed snow that had collected on the soles of our boots. We opened the thick glass doors and advanced to the box office. It felt uncomfortably warm in the theatre upon entering, but after glancing outside again, I found reason to praise the interior atmosphere. We purchased our tickets and opened a second pair of doors to gain access to the lobby. Even through my boots I could feel the tufts of carpet give under my weight. My mouth moistened and my nose wiggled when I smelled the aroma of melted butter and freshly popped popcorn. We walked past the pop-corn stand and stopped in front of the candy display. There we bought Holloway caramel suckers, our customary purchase, because they lasted longest of all the sweets in the selection. If we found ourselves with a nickel left over, we'd buy licorice. Before we entered the auditorium through a third set of doors, Phil and I vowed that we would not start on our suckers until the show was underway. Rendering this vow before entering the auditorium was a rite we observed every Saturday night at the Majestic.

We strolled about halfway down to the screen before beginning to look for our friends. Most of our classmates sat in the seats a few rows back from the front, the girls sitting in the seats next to the walls where they giggled, glanced at the guys, and were boisterous. It seemed to me that the older an individual was, the farther back he'd sit. Adult and teenage couples headed for the rows in the rear or, more daringly, the balcony.

"Hi, Dan! Hi, Phil!" Dick greeted us when he saw us looking for a place to sit. He had saved us each a seat. We sat down, unhinging the padded, curved seats, and everybody chattered until the curtains began to open—an indication that the show would begin in a moment and a signal to hush. It was great to be part of the crowd, to belong, and be like others. When the advertisements came on, I was thinking how glad I was no one besides Phil and me knew of the frustrating procedure we had to endure in order to be present at the Saturday night show.

The previews revealed that a Gene Autry picture, *Champion at Elkhorn Pass*, was scheduled for next Saturday. Phil leaned over and whispered, "Let's see that!"

"Yah!" I replied enthusiastically, "That's bound to be a great show. Everybody will be going."

ഛ • രു

Etleckers' Cottage

At Etleckers' cottage we did most of our serious fishing and some of our funnest swimming. Prairie Lake was no Walden Pond but for us it was the favorite summer haunt. It was much larger, a mile and a half wide in places and six miles in length. The water wasn't as clear as the spring fed liquid Thoreau drank, fished, bathed in, and reflected upon in his Massachusetts hideaway. "God's Drop" he called Walden. Prairie Lake, which was man made, was our paradise. It harked back to primitive times. The water was green with algae, the shore by the dock had a drop-off six or seven feet out, the cabin was rustic.

Indoor plumbing consisted of a sink and a hand pump that we had to prime to get water pouring out. Out front, between the cottage and the gravel road that wound through resorts and private cottages, a sloped path led to Mrs. Murphy, the outhouse. It was a two-holer. Designed to ensure adequate coverage should things get crowded at the cottage? Or maybe to have a spare in case one hole got too full for comfort? I don't know which. There were plenty of other matters to ponder while occupying the privy. At night or if we were sick, or if we deemed the trek to Mrs. Murphy to be personally insulting or embarrassing, we had an option. We could avail ourselves of the baked blue-and-white enamel chamber pot that resided in the oak commode in a corner of the living room. There was a downside, however. Equipped with a lid that had a handle and a chipped lip, the pot typically made a noise like clashing cymbals when we maneuvered it shut to cover our waste. The clank and its echo made the event less private than if we had girded our loins in the first place, braved the elements, and completed the jaunt to and fro the less clamorous, albeit more odoriferous privy. That way lay solitude. But enough on Mrs. Murphy and her would-be company.

Etleckers' cottage veered toward the quaint rather than the ramshackle. The wood frame building, white with green trim, its shingles in need of repair, was apparently a one-room structure in the beginning, but it had morphosed into a peninsula with all three shores wrapped around by an addition some twelve feet wide and composed totally of multi-pane double-hung windows, which gave a panoramic view of the lake and surrounding cottages, trees, and grass. One shore or side was a kitchen, complete with a propane stove and an icebox. As part of the ritual of going to Etleckers, we'd stop en-route (usually at a Pure Oil filling station in Cameron, kitty-corner from the Chick-o-Dine Drive-In, where Highway 8 intersected with Highway 53; Rice Lake, the original county seat of Barron County, six miles to the left; and Chetek, the portal to Prairie Lake, five miles to the right, the direction to our cabin) to buy a hunk of ice that would last the week. The ice block weighed a lot and required heavy tongs to be raised and then lowered into the hinged top of the white, baked-enameled icebox. The bottom of the ice chest, formed of unpainted corrugated steel, had a plug we could pull to drain off melted ice and clean out the ice chest. No matter at the cottage that water routinely leaked out of the icebox or once in a while overflowed from the pump onto the porcelain sink and grooved countertop unit or that we came in dripping wet in swim suits and bare feet. The plank floor was built to handle abuse. In the kitchen, moreover, linoleum gave waterproof protection, at least on the large yet uncracked areas of the faded yellow-and-orange decorated flooring. The autumnal colors had obviously dictated the choice of yellow for the floral curtains that hung café style in the kitchen and contributed to the coziness of the cottage.

Heat for the cottage, should a rainy day or chilly night cause shivers that heavy quilts on the bedsteads couldn't cure, came from a space heater stationed in the living room, which burned wood we hauled in from a pile alongside the cabin and temporarily stored in a cardboard box labeled Angel Wings Toilet Tissue. We'd stash newspapers nearby to light the fires. Else we could raid Mrs. Murphy. Sears-Roebuck catalogs were kept handy in Mrs. Murphy for use when the toilet paper was depleted or we had forgotten to include it with the provisions we'd put in the trunk of the car.

The middle part of the u-shaped addition fronted the lake and together with the remaining part resembled a large porch. It was furnished with a bright, oil-cloth covered banquet-sized table, a cushioned bench on the window side, and chairs crowded on the other three sides. There we would gather for daily fish-fries and all the trimmings. Rainy days offered views of a rippled surface and a lake magically turned from green to slate-gray. Past the table and on the floor in the corner by the door was a wooden box in which an old one-and-a-half horse Evinrude

outboard motor stood, prop side down, alongside a pair of beat-up oars, several fishing poles, a few odd tools, a mop and a broom, and a red can with the proper mix of oil and gas to fuel the Evinrude.

Beyond the entry door and filling in the remaining part of the enclosed addition were three full size, heavily quilted beds. Two bedsteads were of brass, the third and most remote from the door had walnut head and footboards handsomely wrought in a Germanic style. Three chests of draws flanked the interior wall and left a fairly wide aisle for movement day or night. In the adjoining living room, accessible through a large arched doorway off the middle part of the addition, another large bed as well as a hide-a-bed kept company with two equally creaky rocking chairs and an overstuffed chair that did not match the sofa.

On the wall above the bureau that went with the first bed in the porch, the bed Phil and I always claimed, hung a calendar nearly a decade obsolete picturing Man o' War, Sea Biscuit, and Whirlaway. The last scene admired before lowering the wick on the kerosene lamp on the bureau to darken our sleeping quarters, our dreams took their cue from the horses.

A Chetek boat, named for the nearest town to the lake, a Wisconsin town that still enjoys a fine national reputation for its all wood, multi-sparred, round bottom rowboats, was tied to the dock below. It made queer groaning noises rubbing against the dock as the water lapped the shore. When the lake turned all white caps the rhythm of the boat's knocking and scraping the dock could be heard all the way up to the cottage. Strategically positioned at the end of the dock were three canvas mounts in which one could affix cane poles with worms for bait to take advantage of passive fishing.

In Prairie Lake we didn't have to worry much about blood-suckers. They were thick in Lake Mille Lacs, in northern Minnesota, where we cottaged a week one summer as guests of the Schwartzes. We could count on getting them stuck to both feet in most of the country swimming holes we tried out during stays that Dad and Mom had arranged for us with farmer families in the vicinity when they chose to vacation without us. Prairie Lake sheltered turtles in some low water parts but it was best known for its plentiful fish.

Harry Johns, who lived year round in the next cottage, was generous. He talked funny, sort of like he needed to but didn't want to clear his throat—or remove his pipe. He was extravagant with stories about fishing, phenomena associated with the lake and with the life of a widower, which status he had occupied for over a dozen years, and—oh!—how times had changed. Better than even his stories was the fact that he would let us borrow his Johnson ten-horse-power outboard. At full throttle, it would lift the bow of the boat a good six inches out of the water. All we could muster with the worn out Evinrude was a troll. Still, we have to credit the Evinrude for the many trips it powered us to Treasure Island. Visible a mile or so out to the southeast, looking at the lake from the cottage dining room, the island we had dubbed after the story by Robert Louis Stevenson demanded almost two hours of steady rowing to make it there and back. The Evinrude reduced the trip time by half. By Johnson you could cruise there in a little over ten minutes. Once we got there we could spend hours exploring and adventuring.

Harry informed Dad and us boys that he had met an old man who claimed to know where the original Garden of Eden was located. The spot was not far from where the man himself lived. His hut was situated on a shoal near the dog leg that formed the northern most part of the lake. Sadly, we couldn't go along. Harry and Dad ventured there alone, taking Harry's aluminum fishing boat and his ten-horse-power Johnson. When they returned, Dad told us all about it. The guy was nuts. He claimed to have had a vision in which an angel descended on his dock and declared, apparently in King James English, that the land nearby was holy ground, for it had been the plot chosen by God the Father as Eden. "There," saith the Angel, pointing toward that part of the old man's lot that was his vegetable garden, "He did all the mighty acts recorded in the first chapters of the Book of Genesis." Much of the surrounding land was now a dismal swamp and, in that degenerate condition, stood, the old man argued, as a reminder to all man-and-woman-kind that Adam and Eve and all their lineage were fallen creatures who, if they came to faith and led decent lives, could one day inherit the Kingdom of God.

Dad assured us that most of what the old man said was orthodox, except of course, for the blunder about the location of the Garden of Eden. When we questioned Dad as to whether the old man would go to heaven or hell when he died, Dad said it was all in God's hands but he felt sure the man was devout and deserving of a comfortable place in the hereafter. He refused to elaborate. He did consent to show us where the old man's hut was, however. He did so when we motored over in that direction in our Chetek boat to fish for sunfish at dusk one day in late summer. It was pitch dark when we reached our dock that night, the Evinrude having run out of fuel midway, the mosquitos being quite bad. The cottage never looked so inviting, soft light from the kerosene lamps radiating through the windows, Mom there to greet us with milk and sandwiches, and the big bed begging for company.

∽ • ⌘

Growing Up in a Parsonage

As PKs we weren't only preacher's kids, we were privileged characters. The church and parsonage were, in a way, our extended playground.

The men of First Lutheran, farmers and non-farmers alike, would come out to Brotherhood faithfully the third Tuesday night of the month. After devotions, a brief business meeting, and any special program, such as a male vocal duet or a couple of hymns sung by the Bjugstad Female Quartet, they would throw darts. With the enthusiasm of teams participating in intercollegiate athletics, the Brotherhood at First Lutheran sponsored tournaments and competed with other brotherhoods in the Rice Lake circuit of ELC congregations. Phil and I and Toby Thompson, my best friend, and one or two other pals would take advantage of our PK privilege and raid the church for action on rare nights when no meetings were scheduled. On the sly we'd set up the boards and have our own dart throwing party in the church basement.

Other times when the church was hopelessly empty we'd see who could make it across the most pews upstairs in the nave, a daring balancing act that elicited a creak now and then from a pew showing its age like an old person with arthritis whose bones protested when stirred into motion. Once we got caught in the act. From then on pew hopping was largely history.

The church lawn served well as a playing field for touch or tackle football, batting and pitching practice, and tag. At night it was space commandeered for neighborhood games of hide-and-seek, kick-the-can, captain-may-I, and frying-pan. We chose a dimly lit corner of the lawn or sat on the steps to the side entrance, however, when exchanging ghost stories, they being too scary to relate in total darkness.

One custom at First Lutheran we especially looked forward to was the Christmas Day service. The collection that day, and only that day, was given to the pastor and his family. Dad let us help count it all out on the dining room table. It even beat the sorting of candy on the table after our hauls trick-or-treating on Halloween. This was cash. We'd separate coins in piles and place the bills in stacks. Mostly the offering contained ones but some fives and a few tens were always present. One Christmas there were two twenties in the mix. After the tally, which one year exceeded two-hundred-fifty dollars but was usually about one-hundred-fifty, Dad announced how it would be divvied up. We boys received an amount that was higher than the amounts received by the girls, because we were older and because we were male heirs, which was fitting.

Half of the one-story wing on the east side of our two-story brick parsonage was a room we called and used as a den, otherwise serving as a guest bedroom. The attic in the gable above was extra storage space, but because the small door opening into it from upstairs was off the boys' bedroom it enlarged the space Phil and I had to keep and do secret things. The lower half of the wing was Dad's study. It had a separate front entry. Outside next to the doorway an ornate wrought-iron bracket projected. From the bracket swung a small black sign with white script that read REV. P.E. VAN TASSEL.

That was enough of a signal for parishioners who came to see the pastor evenings or other times he couldn't be found in his office across the street in the church. They would seek him there. That is, if the call were not purely social but of a personal nature. Someone who wanted to discuss or confess to a problem and desired pastoral counseling would come to the study and knock. It was a case of his having hung out his shingle. Passersby noticed.

Among those who sought him out, like a ship in a storm, was an itinerant. The same hobo or tramp—we didn't refer to him as a bum—returned several times over the years. Mother would invite him to join the family for dinner. He'd eat a good meal and tell us where he had been and what he had done since the previous visit. He didn't permit himself to linger too long for, as he informed us with a distant sort of look in his eyes, he had to be hitting the road. It was often the tracks. Like others in the fraternal order of hobos, he hitched a lot of trains in his lifetime.

While he was at the table Mom secreted items into the pockets of his faded old suit coat. She'd slip a New Testament and devotional booklet into one and a few pieces of candy and fruit into the other—feeding him body and soul. I don't know if Dad gave him any cash before he left, but perhaps not, because it was likely to have been squandered on liquor or smoke or both. He couldn't afford the habits and had to depend on luck to find cigarette butts long enough to be worth relighting or else bum a smoke from a stranger. His drinking apparently amounted to an occasional binge, since he didn't have any steady income and was dependent almost entirely on handouts. Through these conversations we came to know vicariously something of the adventures and hardships experienced by him and others like him who were homeless drifters. I wouldn't have minded to trade places with him for a spell, but it would have to be a short spell because I knew I'd soon be eager to resume my adventures at home.

The parsonage supplemented the church for ceremonies of a more private or family nature. Some preferred to have a baby baptized in a more intimate setting than a church service. The same held for marriages. I'm glad no one took advantage of the privacy afforded by the parsonage to request that Dad conduct a funeral service there, however.

The parsonage was also host for Sunday School classes that overflowed before the new addition to the church was built. Likewise, meetings of circles or ladies aid or other such groups were sometimes held there. Mom and Dad entertained loads of company. All of us tended to be gregarious. We children would sit half hidden up the stairway to listen in at times we hadn't been encouraged to join a group in the living or dining room. The most enjoyable get-togethers were when our family alone or with relatives or in company with friends monopolized the parsonage. The other occasions, though church-related, felt rather formal and businesslike. I suppose I could be glad I didn't grow up the son of a mortician or a dentist who worked out of his home. Maybe then I'd have joined the hobo for a long stretch of traveling.

We'd play school or doctor at home but when we got the chance we'd play church in the church proper. When our cousins, the Substads, visited us from Minneapolis, we pulled out all stops. We did so literally when we had an opportunity at the Poskin church, which was a small country church included in my dad's parish for a few years till attendance dwindled and it was closed in a merger arrangement with the Barron church. The old pedal pipe organ was fun to play. You could pump out circus music as well as Sunday School songs. Our life was always a mix of the secular and the scared. When Substads came there were enough of us to cover all bases for baseball games and all offices of the church. We'd rotate preaching from the pulpit and pretending to serve communion.

Nobody wanted to play choir or offer special music or give an unsolicited testimony, a practice not condoned by Lutherans but relished by the fundamentalist sects. We could play usher, Sunday School superintendent or teacher, the janitor, or lay reader. All the props (except Prop, of course) were there for a genuine service—hymnals, candles, you name it. We'd perform mock weddings, funerals, baptisms, and, though they were out of character for Lutherans, occasionally we'd conduct a revival. The confirmation ceremony flopped because it was too hard to think up questions to trick the wannabe confirmands. Plus, without white robes and corsages it didn't look convincing.

Don't get me wrong. It wasn't all fun and games. Saturday afternoons we had to fold and stuff bulletins. Mom had her work cut out for her too; she spent an hour or two beforehand at the local REA headquarters typing the stencils to run off the bulletins we then folded on the dining room table. A greater responsibility yet was to be role models. Our decorum was subject to public criticism. Gossip travels fast in a small town. And if a tidbit concerned the preacher's kid it moved especially fast from mouth to mouth, phone to phone. Thus, we were constantly reminded by our parents to behave ourselves. Aren't all children admonished to do so by their parents? Yes, but not with as high a level of expectation that they better be obeyed. Going to church services we had to dress up like everybody else, but in addition we had to refrain from chewing gum, laughing, and any cutting up or fidgeting. We had too much energy to sleep, unlike a few grownups I had noticed over time who religiously dozed off during sermons. They might even have fallen asleep during the Sermon on the Mount, had they been born back then, I mused while watching them sit there, eyes closed and content in their oblivion. Had it not been for our being such active children, I'm certain we'd have been warned not to drowse. Our sinning didn't tend to be of the passive sort. Nor did we belong to the set of sinners who sin intentionally. Our mistakes weren't planned; they just happened. We felt like we were being blamed for an accident.

On the fun side were rummage sales. Because we lived close to the church and were the minister's kids, we'd get over early and get first crack at things for sale. The fish pond, a stand where one gave the lady ten cents and threw a line over the curtain behind which another lady attached a packet to the line, was usually a gyp. Over the years—I kept returning thinking, like a gambler at Vegas, that I'd hit it big one day— I pulled out a pair of gray work socks, a pack of bubble gum, a miniature dog figurine, a thimble and pin cushion, and some other junk I've forgotten it was so bad. We got free cake and ice cream before leaving the sale, which kind of made up for the loss at the fish pond.

The preacher's family was allowed (strike that) expected to join potlucks at Ladies Aid meetings. Their potlucks were on the scale

47

required for threshing crews, so you never left hungry. That was true for congregational dinners as well. Between church dinners and invitations to farm parishioners for Sunday dinners and Ladies Aid potlucks, not to mention pancake suppers and other stuffers, I didn't starve.

WDS. Dad used initials a lot. WDS, "we don't starve," was a favorite. NG he didn't invent, but we knew that one early on. DVBS he would sing over and over again on mornings we had to rise and shine and head off to Daily Vacation Bible School. I enjoyed DVBS, especially when I was in the lower grades and it was held at Ward School and not in the church basement. We could climb out the big windows and walk, feet splayed out, around the building on a stone ledge, holding on to the window trim where we could. The same tall swings that we ran to save during recess during school days were also there for breaks during Bible School sessions. Flannelgraph board presentations, work books in which we wrote answers to questions based on material covered in the book and which had pictures to color and points to connect, like Paul's missionary trips, and the minister's (my dad's) telling a Bible story at the start of the half-day session—these things I liked.

Later on, as adolescents, our attention wandered and we were more minded to pull pranks. One time Toby and I got into trouble when we tried to shame Lois Smathers because she couldn't get all the books of the Bible right. What we did was make up a book, Ichabod, we called it, and to prove its inclusion, invented a verse which we quoted: "Thou, Ichabod, why stoopest so low to the scum of the earth?" We almost got her believing it and including Ichabod in the blanks to be filled in in that section of the workbook dealing with the names of the books in the Bible. The trick was nasty insomuch as Lois was a little odd and so nervous as to be super bashful, engage in peculiar gestures, and talk in a squeaky voice. She had a brother in worse shape who was schooled at home, to the extent that a retarded child can learn. I've been on both sides of teasing but fortunately I was popular and normal enough as a child not to be a subject of teasing. Life does have some regrets, but it takes time to develop a regret. I have to admit I had no regrets at that time over our teasing Lois.

I guess I had outgrown Bible School and LCR (Lutheran Children of the Reformation), an organization we attended after school. There we delighted in singing songs learned in Sunday School, including three of my favorites. They were "Into My Heart," "I Love to Tell the Story," and "Boys and Girls for Jesus." It was evidently time to move on to confirmation and Bible Camp and the flirtations and higher level instruction that accompanied those experiences. We would learn new songs.

None of us had yet heard or seen "Time's winged chariot hurrying near." That would wait for 1955.

For our family the most unforgettable Sunday in Barron was the Sunday Dad announced his resignation. Earlier that week Dad had drawn us all together as a family and informed us that he and Mother had "prayerfully decided to leave Barron and take on a new challenge at a church in Sioux City, Iowa." It was the first Sunday of October. Dad had asked us to keep our news a secret from friends the previous week. Phil and I sat in the balcony next to Sunday School friends. We knew what was coming and waited, our hearts beating almost with guilt of betrayal for not having even hinted anything to our closest friends. After he ended the sermon, Dad paused and then began, "Every once in a while in the life of a pastor and a congregation an important change occurs. Such a change is occurring for me and for First Lutheran. At the close of this calendar year, having been called by God and this congregation ten years ago to serve as the pastor, I will be ending my service here. I have accepted a call to become pastor at First Lutheran in Sioux City, Iowa."

Already Toby was staring at me in shock. "You're leaving Barron?" he whispered in astonishment.

"Yup, we're moving," I returned in words barely audible and bordering on failed self-assurance. Three months later, we sat up there again for Dad's farewell sermon. We spent our last Christmas in Barron and, a week later, our first New Year's in Sioux City. Life in Barron had suddenly become only memories.

Television and Radio

I t was a long time before my dad gave in. We talked and cajoled till it happened. On trips to the Twin Cities where we Christmas shopped in the snow, we'd stroll past the store windows at Donaldson's and at Dayton's, each department store decorated for the holidays and vying for the most elaborate mechanized figures. Behold! Snow White and her Seven Dwarves, Santa and his reindeer, Donald Duck and a raft of other Walt Disney characters, Nativity scenes of animals and biblical figures, ranging from cattle and camels to shepherds, angels, wise men, and the holy family, Frosty the Snowman, favorite characters from the novels of Charles Dickens, especially his "Christmas Carol." Intermittent windows displayed merchandise: new board games, sports equipment and attire, bicycles, erector sets, sewing machines, and, most alluring, television sets all turned to the same channel.

In the late 1940s and early 1950s, television, even when hooked up close to the transmitting stations, gave "snowy" reception. Because the tubes those days imaged exclusively in black and white, the snow effect erased some of the picture. But we could hear what was being said and we saw enough to get the idea. In remote locations like Barron, ninety miles northeast of the Cities by road and, say, seventy miles the way the crow flies, we had to have an antenna to get decent reception. (By definition "decent" included a certain amount of snow.) The antenna, a device designed to fan out wing-fashion to catch and maximize reception from the respective television signal, braced so that its small end faced the Cities, was either attached to a tower secured to the ground by cables or else perched on the rooftop and supported by guy wires at the corners. A spool of television tape, which antedated cable technology, unwound from the antenna to make connection to the set inside. The brown tape slunk along the roof and down the side of the house, threaded its way through special eyelets, snaked through an aperture drilled into the foundation, crawled along the basement joists, and coiled through a hole drilled in the floor to enter the living room. In those days houses didn't have family rooms, though some incorporated dens which, though they were smallish, served a similar purpose.

Mr. Russell, who lived up the street from us and who was always changing jobs or, as a gossipy neighbor put it, "chasing rainbows," had taken up a new career opened by the advent of television. We got him to install our antenna. In the process he came into the house several times for hot coffee and to warm his hands. We wanted to treat him with respect, for we were eager to have the results of his labor turn out right and as fast as possible. The Magnavox with a seventeen-inch screen had been purchased as a belated family Christmas present by Mom and Dad at the local radio and television shop, owned and operated by a man with two highly trained arms but only stumps where there should have been legs. He worked and fronted the counter from a cushioned stool and walked with his hands, his torso swinging like a pendulum. In our family one couldn't just get things out of the blue; one had to count them as gifts for events like birthdays or holidays. And whenever possible, we supported home town businesses.

Television, an expanding enterprise, had become the talk of the town. And now the Van Tassels were in the vanguard, while other folks took up the rear. Opinions about television varied, the minority holding the view of skeptics but the majority coveting the new toy and placing a TV set on their shopping list for next Christmas.

Phil and I palled with Fred and Charles Stair. Like us they were PK's and were about a year apart in age. Their father, a Baptist minister, prided himself on adhering to the literal truth of the Scriptures. In his sermons and prayers at morning and vesper services and in testimonies with the unsaved hither and yon, he harangued on the entire array of sins being committed daily and nightly by practically every soul in and beyond Barron County. The Reverend Stair did not limit restrictions to the Decalogue. No, siree! He went further. He forbade actions and objects galore: dancing (which activity we Lutherans similarly frowned on), smoking (regarded then not so much as a health issue as a sure sign of defiant worldliness), cursing, dark lipstick and heavy makeup (which are bound to promote seduction and ultimately bring grief and remorse), card playing (inevitably leading to gambling and attendant vices), boy scouts, lodges, strong drink, and movies.

When television was invented, he added it to the list of no-no's. He made it known that he prayed harder for people who owned television sets, be they parishioners, the unchurched, Roman Catholics, or Protestants of the errant denominations. I believe he thought the set itself was evil, whether it was plugged in and operating or just sitting there being quiet.

Despite all mischief and ignominy thought to emanate from television, but only after a long campaign launched by all members of the family, and fought most valiantly by Mom, in January 1953, we unpacked a television set at 15 West La Salle Avenue, directly opposite the First Lutheran Church, formerly of the Norwegian synod, where every Sunday we sat in pews shared with a church full of other sinners and saints, many of whom had turned or were turning to television as an answer to their prayers for something good, something new and different, to occupy their leisure time and still be "acceptable in thy sight, O Lord."

Blinds partially pulled shut, the room dimmed with only a so-called television lamp on top of the set, our family gathered in a semi-circle. Not a time of religious devotion or abundant conversation, early

53

sessions spent watching the box nonetheless brought our family and many like it closer together. The marathon began. *I Love Lucy* followed by Ed Sullivan, followed by incredible wrestling matches, followed by *This Is Your Life*, followed by Jackie Gleason and *The Honeymooners* and then wrapped up with news, weather (for "Nodak, Sodak, Minn, Wis, and I"), and sports. *Truth or Consequences*, *You Were There*, Red Skelton, Liberace, Kookla, Fran, and Olly—there was something for everybody.

Early TV started the craze of fixation with monitors that led to today's ubiquitous personal computer, a gizmo capable of accessing all manner of games and fascinating resources available on the Internet. The advancement in our household, as in countless other households, to color TV, when it became affordable and had the bugs worked out a decade later, constituted a mere skirmish. The epic battle had previously been won on a field of black and white. Eventually the Stair family too succumbed, but the war waged in that household took considerably longer and required an order of artillery higher than that needed to win the war in most families. There aren't many conscientious objectors out there now. Today, to note a twist of irony, many an evangelist has embraced the media, especially television, as a pulpit for condemning the exact same things, excepting television sets, that appeared on the list of things impugned by the Reverend Stair of Barron, Wisconsin.

Before that watershed event occurred in our lives, even before we went visiting in order to see television in action at other more progressive, less discriminating households, we were entertained and instructed by another marvel: the radio. The era of radio shows is past. It was glorious in its day. The ears registered the sound, the imagination created the picture.

A bunch of us would race over to Bucky Crowell's after school let out to make it by four o'clock to listen to *B-Bar-B Riders*. The sounds themselves were the "effects." For us, filtering through our consciousness, the sound effects magically became the show. We hardly had time to take our ears off the presentation to indulge in a snack. We sat transfixed. On Saturday nights we wouldn't miss *Back in the Saddle Again*, with Gene Autry, one of whose movies we probably had seen Friday night a week or two back.

Prior to television, audiences "listened" to "shows" on the radio. It wasn't "watching." Besides listening to the "soaps" of that day, like *Our Miss Brooks*, people listened intently to ball games announced play by play. Children tuned in precisely at ten o'clock Saturday morning to listen to Story Hour, sponsored by Cream of Wheat. At midday housewives dusted furniture and listened to Arthur Godfrey joke about the scanty presence of chicken—"Did they just caper through the liquid?"— in the chicken noodle soup processed by Campbell soup, the sponsor of his program. Listeners would strain to hear the names of those selected and tunefully invited "to take your seat in the Lemac Box" (Camel, the sponsor spelled backwards) and later relax by listening to the enjoyable music of the Maguire Sisters. People would listen to Amos and Andy and laugh. People would sit on the edge waiting for the next telltale sounds of a mystery program. People would cry and choke up at the illusions prompted by the radio waves broadcasting matters that came to matter in their own lives. Grown-ups, who would routinely tune in to Cedric Adams on WCCO for the evening news, welcomed the opportunity to put a face with the familiar lilting voice when he came up from Minneapolis to appear as the main celebrity at the Barron Butter Festival one summer. Pre-television entertainment spoke, sang, and made sound for a blind audience that saw everything in its collective mind's eye.

Little wonder Garrison Keillor revived the radio program format and succeeded in attracting live audiences and airwave audiences, going on to transform those avid listeners into spellbound readers of his stories chronicling the lives of men, women, and children from Lake Wobegon. His is the kind of news that radio is particularly good at portraying. Such script suits radio and audience alike.

Mishaps

For a family of eight, counting parents and Mary Jane, a tail-ender born the year after we got television, not to have suffered any broken bones was remarkable for that day . . . or any day. We had our scrapes and illnesses like everybody else, but, except for Connie and me, no one could call us accident prone. I was the one who had to leave Scout camp early after burying a hatchet in my shin. Connie was the one who spilled hot gravy on herself and burned herself pretty badly. I ran into a parked car on my bike one day while daydreaming and not paying attention to anything but the fact that I was proudly riding no hands. The cuts and bruises I got from that encounter, flying off my bike as it hit the bumper and scraping myself on the sidewalk up the bank from the curb, together with the embarrassment I suffered, conspired to keep me more attentive of where I was going from then on. The day my rear bicycle tire blew up when I was filling it at the Pure Oil station after patching a flat was a freak thing as well. My cheeks were red from the impact and humiliation. Connie had the record for stubbed toes. Carole came hobbling home from Sharon Cubbine's one day after slicing her foot on a hoe. Phil has a scar on his forehead from hitting the corner of a chest of drawers getting out of the bunk in the dark. A stray dog we befriended, Mops, got hit by a car once, but fortunately he bounced off the front wheel with only a cut and a whimper.

When cousins had come to visit and we were downstairs roller skating in the basement, I happened to bang into a steel support pole. The bump on my forehead was big and would soon become black and blue. Mom intervened. She came to the rescue with a large knife, which because of its inherent coldness would reduce the swelling. But I thought she was planning to cut the bump off and yelled out in fright and desperation, "Please don't! It's okay. I'm all right!"

From time to time Mom would say, "Think of what could have happened," when we related our latest adventures. Yes, we could have drowned crossing the walk-over bridge in the park hand-over-hand on the supporting cables suspended beneath. Yes, we might have fallen from the tree top. Yes, guns are dangerous. How we survived and escaped hurt was astonishing.

It was a good twelve feet from the top of the railing on the slanted garage roof that was built to serve as a patio off a doorway on the landing going upstairs. We'd pile snow hip high below on the other side of the driveway and then race up to jump. We leapt as if it were the high dive at the park and water instead of snow we'd be landing in. In the summertime, shouts of "Anty-I-Over" flew with the ball over the garage as makeshift tournaments filled intertudes of fun-packed action.

Once when the baby sitter was with us I took advantage of the time to fool with the washing machine in the basement. Perhaps I was seven, going on eight.

Fascinated with the wringer, I ran some rags through it, the same way Mom would slip wet clothes through it to squeeze out the wash water. We knew how to set up the wash and had helped many times. Mainly she had us shave off pieces of Fels Naphtha to use during those years when she refused to buy Oxydol because of the price difference. When my finger caught on a rag I was feeding into the wringer it took but a few seconds for my hand and then my arm to follow. At my elbow the machine balked and I yelled. Downstairs came the sitter to see what was the matter. Phil followed her. Good thing. Because he knew, as she did not, how to release the wringer. I did too but was too horrified to react. It left a burn and a scar, which for many years I obediently showed people when Mom or Dad would bring up the incident with visitors. There are those times when everyone is sharing their experiences, each one contributing a story. "Now, I've got one that beats that," some one would throw in and then relate the anecdote, like different musical instruments playing variations on a theme. "Danny, show us your elbow."

Then there was the time in Minneapolis on a streetcar. Phil and I were independent, sitting there each at a window. Mom and Carole were back a couple of seats. There weren't any bars on the windows and I had been busy looking at things as we clanged along the street. Evidently I got my head out too far when staring at something. I felt a weird sensation. I put my hand to my head above my right eye, got up, and walked back to Mom. Without a word from me, she took charge. The streetcar driver was immediately informed of the accident. We stopped. By a stroke of luck—we needed a little by that time—there was a medical clinic on the very block where the streetcar had stopped. The doctor sewed up the gash with eight stitches. Later, as we told the story, including the part about the truck parked along the curb with a large side mirror that stuck out too far—or was it my head that stuck out dangerously far?—I had to bend over and put my head forward, not to recreate the incident but to allow the audience to see the scar.

As teenagers, Phil and I and four other friends riding in a 1953 Ford station wagon, with Fred Stair at the wheel, rolled when rounding an icy curve on the Poor Farm Road, just past the city dump. Till then we had been enjoying the way the car was careening along, swaying and skidding on the unsanded road, now and again briefly out of control. When Fred approached the curve, however, he jammed the brakes, hoping to pilot the craft to a speed more negotiable. From the crown of the road we glided onto the snow-covered shoulder and sailed into the snow-packed ditch like a dinghy with its daggerboard having already been pulled up but its sails unfurled too late to keep it from colliding into a dock.

For the second or two that the vehicle slid on its roof, we had the sensation of being in the rocket ride on the midway at a carnival when the thing twisted upside down and we felt all discombobulated and ready to puke. The beams of the headlights, the sparkling stars overhead, and the glare of the light pole straight for which we were headed blent with the faint glow of a yard light in the distance, where a farmer and his wife were just bedding down for the night. When the car stopped, I peered out through the gap that resulted from the door on my side being wrenched from its upper hinge from the impact. I was dusted with snow and my lip was bleeding. In the very back, Dave was complaining of a lump on his arm. Fred exclaimed, "Oh, my God! Don't tell my dad!" as he swung around to check that no one was missing or dead and flung open the driver's side door to inspect the damage.

The Ford sat upright just inches from the light pole, its V-8 motor still humming. At first Fred thought all was right and shouted, relieved, "Let's tramp back to that farm and see if they'll pull us out with a tractor."

By that time we had all crawled out of the car and were comparing views of what exactly happened and how we felt. Phil ran his hand over the roof. "She feels like corduroy, Fred. And," he went on, pointing to the right rear panel, "she'll need serious body work."

That night the farmer whose yard light we followed, like sadder but wiser versions of the wise men of old, went to bed a little later than usual. His tractor stayed in the shed and his cows got milked on schedule, at 5:00 a.m. But his telephone was off the hook for the few seconds it took Fred to call his dad and tell him we'd wrecked on the Poor Farm Road. The marvel is that the Reverend Stair didn't end up in a snowbank himself, he got there so fast in the car borrowed from a deacon who lived right next door to the Baptist parsonage. We spotted the headlights as we stepped out of the farmer's house, having forgotten to thank him for the use of his telephone. Earlier, a few "Thank God!"s had been uttered, when we realized and appreciated that none of us had been seriously injured. Fred's dad drove us home, en route reconfirming his belief in a providential God and expressing his amazement at the fact that the car had missed the pole and was still running.

The next day was school so we didn't get to go back to the scene to see the tracks we had made or watch the tow truck haul the vehicle to the body shop. A big consolation for Fred was that he didn't get cited for reckless driving and that his dad suspended his driving privilege for merely the time it took to repair the wagon.

§ • ⁂

Christmas by the Book:
A Translation from Norwegian

T he rule on Christmas Eve was that we had to wait till the cross on
the church tower went on before unwrapping presents. The cross
was timed to light precisely at seven. Before sitting down to supper we'd start glancing in that direction and afterwards we'd all keep a pretty steady vigil or take turns checking and periodically reporting, "Not yet!"
until the blue cross appeared in sight through the picture window. The window was a kaleidoscope. It reflected the string of colored lights outside
woven into the evergreen garland surrounding the window and the light
from a flood light placed on the lawn to illuminate an angel figure and a
sign that spoke of glad tidings. Like a double-exposure photo, the plate
glass at the same time refracted the lights strung on the tree inside, some of
them prismatic glass candles that bubbled. The glow of the little lights, in
turn, played off the tinsel and shiny ornaments that hung on the tree. The
presents heaped on the floor below added color and mystery. We all had a
hand in trimming the tree, decorating the house, and getting and wrapping
gifts, mostly using the paper and ribbons Mom saved from Christmases
past. She took care of festooning the corner cupboards in the dining room
with bows of evergreen. Poinsettias, an advent wreath, and the flame and
scent of candles made the house a living Christmas card.

During the holidays in our house we listened to carols from the record player and, off and on, from Mom playing the piano, the same tunes heard over and over in stores, in church services, on the streets, and over the radio. But they didn't wear out. Instead they sharpened the focus and raised the spirits. Added to the repertoire at First Lutheran were the Norwegian carol *"Jeg er så glad"* and, in the spirit of ecumenism, the German version of an old favorite, *"Stille Nacht, heilige Nacht."* But English prevailed.

What we ate for Christmas Eve supper and Christmas Day dinner was totally different from what we ate day to day, Sundays included. Unique to the Scandinavian heritage transported to the upper Midwest by immigrants settling there at the turn of the century, food at Christmas time was no common fare. We acquired a taste for the dishes making up the smorgasbord at the same time we learned to pronounce their funny names. To make them we had to have recipes faithfully handed down for generations, special cookery, utensils we'd stash away the rest of the year and dig out as Christmas approached, and the right ingredients in the right proportions. It was deemed best when done in the old-fashioned way on a wood-fired iron stove. *Julekake* (sweet bread with currants), *lefse* (imagine a tortilla made with potatoes and buttered and sweetened with brown sugar before being rolled), *fattigmann bakkels* ("poor man's cookies"), rosettes, *lutefisk* (indescribable boiled fish that is twice netted, once when caught and again, with cheesecloth, when cooked), boiled potatoes, pickled herring, and *frukt suupe* (heated fruit pudding).

Lefse Mom would make other times of the year as a surprise, but *lutefisk* was on the table only once a year. Strangers who dared to sample *lutefisk*, out of curiosity or in concession to hospitable coaxing ("yist t'rye a morsel, ja betcha"), would say thank you politely and silently conclude, with a grimace, that it was a once-in-a-lifetime thing, not ever wanting to see, smell, or least of all taste it again. The trick was to be Norwegian. Then, naturally, a person joined in out of loyalty, perpetuating the bravery of the Vikings whose deeds were recounted in ancient sagas. We were carrying on family traditions of generations of

Scandinavians from the old country whose lifestyle, greatly calmed down from that of the wild Danes who plundered, drank, swore, and fought with abandon, was thought to be superior to everybody's but Adam and Eve before the Fall.

After the pageant, which was held at church on a night a few days in advance of Christmas, the Sunday School teachers handed out to those children in their class sacks loaded with ribbon candy, chocolates, peanuts, and a Delicious apple wrapped in a purple tissue stamped Washington State. It was the finale, a word we always used to describe the burst of fireworks ending the Fourth of July celebration in the park. The sacks were the last course. The first course was a brief children's sermon by the pastor, followed by congregational singing of carols, the lighting of the Advent candles, and the program.

Each class and each child had a part, some forced to recite pieces and wear bathrobes and other costumes to recapture the story of the manger baby that changed the world. Another Christmas hymn, most likely either "Oh, Come All Ye Faithful" or "Joy to the World," a prayer, and then the sacks. Except for the change of names in the cast, the script each year was a carbon copy of the one the year before. But it never seemed redundant.

On the secular side, we paid homage to Santa Claus. I remember the moment that bubble burst. Bill Meisegar, an old parishioner from the Poskin church who enjoyed bringing fresh fish to the parsonage, pail after pail of sunfish caught in Lake Vermillion as he filled out his days of retirement, had stopped by the house. He was dressed as Santa. In his regular togs, he formed a jolly roly-poly figure. So he wasn't really out of character. Still, we children didn't recognize him when he stood at the door with a bushel basket of presents he'd come to deliver. Wait! I saw among the packages a gift I had bought and wrapped myself for Mother. "How did that get mixed in?" I wondered. Then my little mind graduated. It was an epiphany. I could no longer believe in Saint Nick. The jig was up. Our parents had been duping us, as have and will other mothers and fathers and aunts and uncles for time out of mind.

Many parishioners brought tributes. Farmers with cuts of meat butchered from well-fed stock, hunters with venison steak, folks with produce from their gardens pressure-cooked into Ball jars, church members and non-church members alike delivering or sending greeting cards with handwritten messages of gratitude for the minister and his fine family, every once in a while one with a five- or ten-dollar bill enclosed, and women stopping by with home-cooked dishes. Louie Olson, who managed Erickson's Grocery, named after his father-in-law, could be counted on for wonderful surprises such as baskets of Texas grapefruit or, one year, a large blanket from Faribault Woolen Mills.

The inventory of gifts exchanged at school, Sunday School, and among our family went way beyond boxes of chocolate covered cherries, assorted flavors of Life Savers and chewing gum, and puzzles. We went all out at home. Socks, shirts, hankies, sweaters, board games, dolls, hand-decorated wooden plates crafted at school in secret, toys of all sorts, books, sports equipment, perfume—the scene in the living room after the presents had been opened resembled an emporium.

It was nice to be off from school for a stretch during the holidays. We had time to hit Quaderer's Creek with our new skates or try out a hill with the sled that we just got. We could play Monopoly and work puzzles, read books and try on brand new clothes. While the girls cuddled and dressed and undressed their dolls, jumped rope, or busied themselves with coloring books and paper dolls, we boys could crawl on the floor, spluttering while pushing toy trucks and cars along make-believe roads or go down the basement and plug in the transformer to operate the Lionel train set or experiment with the wood-burning set. With our best friends we didn't wait till back in school to share what we got for Christmas.

Ice Skating and Frolicking in the Snow

Good times at the skating rink. To put on our skates—we mostly had hockey skates, though girls preferred figure skates—we'd sit on the tailgate of what's-his-name's converted hearse or inside the warming house on benches. The place glowed from the fire stoked in the makeshift fifty-five-gallon drum stove. Chatter, shouts, laughter, music blaring inside and out, sometimes waltzes but more often rock-and-roll, and chronic clicking of skate blades blended cacophonously, creating an atmosphere that could match the most raucous of German beer gardens. The rink was a patch of land flooded by volunteer firemen and frozen by the arctic effect caused by the earth's tilt. The rink's location being so convenient to the new football field meant that the snack shack could be opened for skating nights. Cups of hot cocoa augmented the warmth generated by wearing longjohns and wool socks. Walking home, skates tied together and slung over our shoulder, our feet tingled and, as was true after roller skating, felt unguided and still elevated. By the time we broke out in a run, however, they had become adjusted to life and terrain outside the rink.

We speculated that if we practiced skating and took it seriously, we too could participate in the celebrated Ice Capades. But what fun is that? We had it all in our own backyard.

While we didn't flood our backyard as some folks did, making a trip to the town rink unnecessary and simultaneously building neighborhood spirit, we often headed off to the creek. If the snow were light on the ice, skating could commence at once. If a blanket of snow covered the ice, kids took turns shoveling off a widening area till a glistening dance floor appeared. Or, for greater adventure, with our blades we cut a trail that meandered miles, here and there momentarily halted by a large stone or fallen tree limb. In the light of the sun during the day or by the light of the stars and the moon at night, we celebrated the magic of gliding on the creek.

We did not need ice to have fun. Snow sufficed. When new fallen and wet, snow could be packed into a ball. One option was to roll the ball across the surface, pushing and guiding it to pick up snow and momentum, switching directions so that the snowball kept its spherical shape (or at least continued as a rounded cube) as it expanded layer by layer. To build a snowman, we'd form two proportional snowballs for the body, mount a smaller third snowball atop to serve as the head, pack and shape snow into arms, and complete the creation by adding coal lumps or stones for eyes, sticks for details, and, for greater verisimilitude and as a gesture of friendship, an old hat, a scarf, and mittens. *Voila!*

An alternative was to roll and join snowballs to define walls to simulate a house or stack them solid for a fort. With enterprise and happily volunteered labor, a tower could arise in a couple of hours. The night's cold aided in preserving the monument. Thawing and freezing, repaired as required, a fort could hold out for weeks, all the while providing the scene for war games.

Our versions of arctic architecture varied. Either with snowballs or hunks of crusty snow carved out with mittened hands, we would fashion an igloo. The dome part was the hardest to construct. But never mind. The roof feature could be skipped and just imagined. Purposeful adventure prevailed whether the edifice were big or small, sprawled or tall.

Putting aside frigid construction projects and escapades of sledding, skiing, skating, and tobogganing, another delight snowballs fostered were fights. Not methodically determined by counting off by twos, as in dividing up into teams for softball or baseball, the sides for snowball fights sprang up spontaneously. Sometimes a fight erupted by a chance snowball that hit harder than was considered fun.

Steven and David Coon, whose corner-lot house sat conveniently on a block adjacent to Ward School, stood their ground—snowy ground—one evening as a quartet of boys pelted them with snowballs. The brothers, who were frequently picked on at school, recruited their father to offset the number ganged up against them. Leonard Coon, though not a large man, hauled milk for a living and consequently was strong armed. He could throw well and, in a few minutes of frosty volley, changed the course of the battle. Instead of declaring retreat, our side gave in. Fun turned from lobbing snowballs to drinking a round of hot cocoa brought out by Thelma, the boys' mother, an excellent cook and, when a new zippper had to be sewn on a jacket or the worn collar of a shirt had to be reversed for extended use rather than relegated to the rag bin, the town's most talented seamstress.

Another night's snowball fight ended less well. Roger Hyle, who lived in a half-finished rock-veneered house a few blocks from school, received a snowball in the face that led to his becoming blind in one eye. The identity of the culprit who packed ice or gravel into the renegade snowball was never divulged; the hostile snowball couldn't be singled out from the hail of snowballs that caught Roger's backside, front, arms, and head. Usually, because winter garments by nature are thick or padded for warmth, a kid was protected against any permanent injury to body or pride. Sadly, not so that night, however.

We would lie supine in a field of pristine snow, sweep arms back and forth, then get up and trudge a little ways off: behold, an angel! Making angels in the snow, marking out a large-sliced pie for fox-and-geese, tramping out letters to form names or simple messages—snow, the highlight of a season, provided a palette for the imagination and a release for the boundless energy of youth. Sometimes, shoveling sidewalks or driveways paid off in the treats gained by such labor. In our winter wonderland, chores were outnumbered by frolics.

School Days

I didn't *like* school. I *loved* it. To be inside in a high-ceilinged classroom with light globes chasing the shadows away, the old wall clock ticking, faces of George Washington and Abraham Lincoln peering down approvingly, the alphabet in big Palmer script above the blackboard, sitting in desks with inkwells and scratched initials from the past on the surface and with room inside to sequester a treat, all your books, an Indian Chief tablet, and a cigar box containing colors, pencils, erasers, and milk money—what could be more cozy on a cold winter's day?

Along with Francis Matson, Allen Taft, Mary Viitanen, and Charles Quaderer, I was a fast reader and could pronounce words that would stump most average students. Miss Adams, who taught second grade, would divide her pupils into circles, ensuring a mix of reading levels in each, and the groups would compete for speed and accuracy. That's how we got through our primers, from Dick and Jane onwards.

Ward School had tube slides for fire escapes. They connected to the second floor classrooms through special round flap doors. When we had drills, we'd get to evacuate in the funnest possible way, by sliding, two or three at a time, as if riding a toboggan, to the bottom and then gathering in safety out by the fence alongside the tracks. When school was not in session we could climb up inside the tubes by spreading our feet and putting pressure on both sides and then squeezing our backs against the top to inch our way up. At the top, we'd yell "Bombs away!" and sail down the smooth steel on our butts. Without a teacher or class monitor at the top coaching us to go slowly, the momentum at the bottom would fling us several feet clear of the slide, and we'd have to spring to our feet and run a ways to keep from falling down on our backs.

The swings in the playground were so high we thought it might be possible to shoot right over the bar to which the chains were attached. But when we pumped ourselves almost level with the bar, we'd let loose and bail out, crashing to the leaves or snow piled up below. A jungle gym, trapeze bars, and a row of teeter-totters, coupled with all the laughter and clanking, helped turn recesses into a circus. On the other side of the schoolyard was space for kickball and softball, pump-pump-pull-away, and king-of-the-hill. In the spring, as the snow melted we'd wade in the ditches and storm drain till the water reached into our boots. Then we'd get to go to the basement where the janitor, Alex Gullicson, would let us sit on the floor in the furnace room to dry off. Every fall before it started to snow, he'd paint our initials on our boots so we could keep track of them.

When the grass came back to replace the mud left after thawing, we'd play marbles. We were warned not to play for keeps because that would be gambling, which was illegal and sinful. When we got better at the game and were able to keep and not lose our choice steelies when we shot, we would break the law and succumb to the temptation to play for keeps. I wondered if criminals got their start at school. After all, with all the rules there, one could expect that some would be broken and that corruption might become rampant. Still, as I thought more about it, I concluded that there were a lot worse places to be growing up than the school grounds.

An area in the basement, next to where Blanche prepared lunch, was set up with low tables and benches. If we brought our own lunch we were to remain at our desks upstairs to eat. I bought lunch maybe once a week. What I really liked was the mix of orange and grapefruit juice Blanche served on certain days. Every day in the middle of the morning we had a nutrition break. For a nickel we got a small bottle of milk (our choice, white or chocolate) or orange juice (again, our choice) and half a graham cracker to keep us going the rest of the day. Friday afternoons the teacher picked a student to pass out goiter pills. They came in a round paper container like salt did and were chocolate flavored. When it was our time to pass them out, we could sneak a handful to put in our pocket to retrieve later like candy.

Children aren't always fair, courteous, or the other things the Boy Scout motto upheld. I can vouch for that from the reception I got the day I wore slippers to school. I had raced home for lunch and discovered a birthday package from Aunt Ardis had come in the mail that morning. It was a pair of leather slippers, the kind older men tend to shuffle around in. Well, to my disappointment that afternoon, I was ridiculed instead of envied. I confined my wearing them from then on to when I was relaxing in my—well, Phil's and my—bedroom.

During grade school I must have spent half the time in class preparing posters and bulletin boards and practicing for and competing in spelling bees. All members of our family inherited a talent for creativity and were superior spellers. The teachers recognized that we were budding artists and had orthography down pat. So they called on us to assist with the visuals that people have come to expect in school rooms. Among the exhibition pieces I had a hand in was a beautiful rendition of the Parthenon. Jonathon Topple and I did it with pastel chalks. The sky, since it was located in Greece, sported one fleecy cloud against a backdrop of azure to match the Mediterranean Sea. The columns of the temple were fluted; we copied them from a picture in the *World Book Encyclopedia* that took up a whole shelf next to the radiator. We weren't Romans, but like them we copied the Greeks.

The concept of release time from routine classroom work in order to do enrichment projects, based on one's proven academic performance, carried over into my freshman year of college. My English composition and literature professor gave a diagnostic grammar test early on in the course. A handful of us achieved scores high enough to exempt us from the three-week unit in the syllabus she had devoted to standard grammar and usage. We were presented the alternative of absenting ourselves from that unit during which time we would each read a novel selected from a list she had devised. We would return to her office in three weeks to report on the novel and then resume our seats in the class for the remainder of the semester, writing papers and reading and discussing works of literature, starting with Thomas Hardy's *The Return of the Native*. Fine! My assignment was a novel by Henry James. On the Monday two days before the expiration date of our furlough, I ran into Miss Stolee on the campus. She greeted me and inquired, "Mr. Van Tassel, I see you have volume one of *Wings of a Dove* checked out from Rolvaag Library. I'm guessing you have the other volume in your personal collection?" She let it drop at that. I had to put in an all-nighter to be ready for the conference in her office scheduled for that Wednesday. So we live and learn, as they say.

Time at Camp and in the Scouts

Distant an hour by boat and a half hour by car from Etleckers' cottage, Luther Park Bible Camp occupied acreage fronting Prairie Lake where the beach was sandy and sloped gradually. On a Sunday afternoon in July, we walked down to the lake on a winding path thickly covered with pine needles and shaded by trees. A breeze wafted a pleasant smell of pitch through the branches soughing and swaying overhead. Footfalls and laughter and voices of others arriving disturbed the natural quiet and awakened our social expectations for the week unfolding. Peering ahead through the partially hidden view, we spotted a raft with a diving board and a slide floating on steel drums out past a roped-off crescent of shallower water.

To the left of the swimming area, tied to their anchors and heaved part way up onto the sand, a dozen or more red-and-white rowboats, each with a number stenciled to its bow, rocked hypnotically from small waves and ripples reaching forward and disappearing on the shore. We would be able to sign out a boat for up to an hour and check out a pair of oars and life jackets from the person in charge at the boathouse.

About thirty feet out from where the sterns of the boats were bobbing, as if to soft music, rested a small island overgrown with brush, one of several bog islands on the lake. The narrowness of the channel between the island and the shore line called for some fancy maneuvering when back-paddling out and heading around into open water. Bog islands sort of float, held loosely in place by a tangle of long roots shooting down through a layer of water, some making it to the bottom where they spread out and dig into the sand. Should a Luther Park mariner and his or her mate, accidentally or on purpose, get off course and bump into the bog, to satisfy their curiosity they could slice a way in, pulling with hard strokes on the oars against the thick bramble. However, such a tactic would risk getting locked in as the shrubs and cranberry bushes reclaimed their position, making it difficult to row out. To compound their plight, stepping out of the boat onto the island, one sank immediately. Those who had been to camp before knew about this phenomenon and passed the word, so everybody, the curious and the skeptical alike, eventually came to know, whether by first-hand experience or through hearing from others, to beware the bog. If a guy were out there with a girl and started joking about exploring the island, he might just have to "return to shore immediately!" That could mark the first and last date with the girl and put an end to a voyage to boot.

Fortunately, there were ample grounds for young people to stroll around at camp and hold hands, a pastime calling for a different order of boldness but ensuring dry terrain. Softball and tennis, shuffleboard, volley ball, and ping pong, all popular activities for late afternoon, offered additional alternatives to those desiring a break from water sports.

The campgrounds were wooded but had paths and clearings among the various buildings. Walking up and down the opposite lanes past the girls' and boys' cabins was like reading a map of greater Barron County. Each cabin belonged to a church in the Rice Lake circuit and was marked with the name of the town in which the church resided. The campgrounds became the campers' village, a whole population of teenagers, for the week. Granted, adult supervision was present and a list of rules was tacked to the inside of the front door of each cabin, but still campers were pretty much on their own. The inhabitants of each cabin, housing quite a few friends from home, formed a tightly knit family. Everyone quickly made new friends with others in the neighboring cabins, some of whom it was likely a person would not have to wait till next summer's camp to see again.

Our day at Luther Park followed a schedule. After breakfast the bell was rung a second time, calling all campers to worship. The chapel was a huge log building with flaps on the sides propped up so that when the wide doors were shut we got ventilation through the exposed screen windows. The floor was cement, and curved back wooden seats accommodated row after row of campers. Below the windows sat stacks of folding chairs on the ready should they be needed. No excuse to miss the service. As announced the first day at orientation, "Attendance will be taken at each service (but, don't worry, never an offering, as at services back at your home church)." At morning services and vespers, local and visiting pastors gave inspiring messages and led campers in spirited singing. Mid-morning Bible instruction took place in small groups on benches in shady groves—outside, if it wasn't raining. While our minds might wander or our eyes might rove to try to pinpoint certain campers we were going to be on the lookout for after chapel, the main distractions were the flies that entered through holes in the screens at morning worship and the throngs of mosquitoes that joined the group for lakeside songfests in the evening, an activity that found some campers paired up and holding hands.

During chapel one pastor was assigned to go from cabin to cabin conducting inspection. The tidiest cabin was honored with applause at lunch in the dining hall and as a reward was freed of KP duties the next day. At mention of the name of the messiest cabin, hisses ensued. For being derelict in the domestic realm of camp life the cabin was slapped with KP duty for the remainder of the week. Instead of saying grace at lunch and dinner, tables belted out rounds of "For Life and Health and All Things Good, We Give Thee Thanks, O Lord." Meals ended with "The Doxology" and then a stampede. On the way in, however, lines were expected to be orderly. They were supposed to be equally orderly leaving but never were.

Pouring out of the dining hall past the pump, at which someone was always busy filling the tin pitchers that flashed back and forth from one thirsty table inside to another, campers lingered in earshot in hopes of being included in mail call that day. By the end of the week upwards of half the campers lucked out and heard from a friend or a family member. Many campers jotted a quick line on a postcard picked up with a three-cent stamp at the canteen to send home, some having been pressured to promise to do so when they spilled out of the car at the beginning of camp. Afternoons were "open time" for recreation and rest, the latter option in most cases a throwaway.

A half hour before the curfew to return to the cabins for devotions and to bunk down for the night, the canteen was open. It was a good idea to bring some money to camp, not simply for essentials like toothpaste and shampoo, but in order to load up on treats at the canteen to indulge after lights out before calling it a night.

On a crisp Saturday in early October, the camp site came alive again, not with as vast a number of young Lutherans as during camp week and certainly not because of the menu of activities enjoyed back then. It was time to fulfill a church obligation. Each congregation was represented by a few volunteers to clean, paint, and repair the cabin that belonged to them. If veteran campers happened to be among those joining the cleaning "party," a misnomer appearing in all church bulletins the previous Sunday (and Phil and I, of course, would be joining, as it was expected the minister and his family in each of the congregations would provide the nucleus for the detail group), we'd steal an idle moment to seek out friends, renew ties, and reminisce about the great time we had together at camp week. Then back to our respective cabin to complete the work. Grab a broom and beat the mattresses hauled out for airing, sweep the floors, get a hammer and check outdoor benches for any popped-up nails, fetch the lye for Mom to sanitize the outhouses, and fix whatever needed fixing. Finally, close and shutter the windows. Only then could the cabins hibernate, while school and responsibilities at home preoccupied campers till next summer.

Boy Scout camp offered education and entertainment of a different order. It accentuated the primitive and tribal. Of course there were no girls present to keep a camper from concentrating on things presumably of interest only to boys. Like developing survival skills. We'd learn what roots were edible, how to prepare a bed site with ferns under our sleeping bags when not tenting, what size of an X to cut in the arm or leg and where precisely to tie a tourniquet should a person be bitten by a poisonous snake, what might be required in way of rescue and first-aid procedures, how to light a fire with flint and steel and a wisp of tinder, and the best methods for using a compass to keep our bearings. We were taught what to carry and not carry in a backpack when going on a long hike or camping overnight. Contents should include, minimally, a compass, a hank of rope, a jackknife, a mess kit, a flint-and-steel kit, important grub like a can of beans and packets of powdered rations, a first-aid kit, and a flashlight. We always smuggled in matches rather than delay things after an exhausting hike by making a fire with sticks. We had to remember to fill our canteens; otherwise when we ran out we'd have to scoop water out of the lake or river and boil it. All this and accompanying lore found in the Boy Scout manual lay behind the famous motto, "Be prepared!"

At Camp Phillips, an unending tract of forest located on a lake by the unincorporated village of Haugen, seven miles northeast of Rice Lake and staying south of "Hayward, Hurley, and Hell," as some styled it, we'd put in a week of effort and fun every summer. Our troop would work to set records. Troop #6 is remembered for having had the most cookouts, our first year eighteen out of a possible twenty. That year we had absolutely no recollection of what the mess hall looked like, having taken a quick early breakfast and a late supper there upon arrival, after which our troop, not known at home as being anti-social, cocooned itself at a site in the thick of the woods a mile from the shore of a small lake to address the challenges of living off the land. I was so happy to have real eggs and milk at home when it was all over. Not that we didn't feel proud or weren't fascinated at the fact of our having repeatedly turned powder to liquid and created flames by blowing with all our might on sparks flying onto crumpled leaves.

We lost weight during the week—sweating, working, and cooking out—unless we sissyed out, as we did in subsequent years, and ate most meals at the mess hall. What we gained, though, were more merit badges to add to our sashes. Phil and I were obsessed by the goal of earning every merit badge in the book. By the time we quit Scouts, our sashes were so lit up with colored circles, we could pass for decorated soldiers back from the front lines. Having so many badges emblazoned on our uniforms made us stand out when we marched in the local parades or ushered in church. You name it, there was a merit badge in there somewhere: odd ones like pioneering, pathfinding, and semaphore; easy ones, such as swimming, canoeing, life saving, and camping; hard ones, including knot tying, first aid, and the identification of birds and plants; and those acquired back home, such as bookbinding, animal husbandry, and carpentry.

Although Phil and I did participate in the Order of the Arrow, a ceremony held around a bonfire at night and featuring Indian dances, powwowing, and whooping it up to the rhythmic beating of drums, neither of us succeeded in becoming Eagle Scouts. About the time we would have been expected to achieve the heights of an Eagle, we soared onto other challenges than Scouts. Our interest plateaued when we reached the Star and Life levels. Neither my brother nor I nor most of our friends were too keen on participating in the activities outlined for Explorers, the notch above Boy Scouts, which would have seen us wearing new forest green uniforms and brown neckties.

Before we were done, however, we both earned the coveted Pro Dei et Patria award. "For God and Country." On the civic side, we marched in uniform in the requisite number of parades, learned to fold and fly a U.S. flag correctly, and helped in community efforts such as newspaper drives and litter patrol. In fulfillment of the religious side, we both logged enough hours ushering at church, and I crafted a replica of a church altar while my brother studied so he could enumerate, with the proper architectural terms, the parts that typically make up a church building, or at least those found in cathedrals.

Before donning the characteristic olive-drab uniforms and red kerchiefs of the Boy Scouts, we apprenticed in the blue-and-yellow attire of Cub Scouts. We transitioned into Boy Scouts from Cub Scouts via the link called Webelos. Nobody was to divulge what Webelos actually stood for, that it was an acronym for WE'll BE LOyal Scouts. In practice, it signified that we had made the grade and were enrolled in Boy Scouts, having finished our career in Cub Scouts, moving along in rank from Bobcat, to Wolf, to Bear, and, ultimately, to Lion. We reorganized from pack to troop and from dens to patrols.

Cubs had us doing more in the garage and around town than out in the woods. My favorite Cub Scout project involved making a suit of armor out of tar paper. We cut out the constituent parts, breast plate and all, with tin snips, painted them with aluminum paint, and laced them

together with leather thongs. Swords were silver colored and made of wood. For helmets we reshaped and cut old felt hats and dipped them in the same shiny paint. Finally, we had to surrender an old pair of jeans to the cause to be silverized and worn as leggings under the protective tar paper parts. The outfit looked convincing but it was so stiff from paint we couldn't bend at the elbows and knees. We could barely hobble and, clearly, could not expect to mount a horse, much less ride and joust. Not that we had really counted on a tournament. Yet our mothers were as proud of us in our home-made armor as King Arthur and his court must have been of their knights-in-arms and their deeds of derring-do back in medieval times.

While Cub Scouts didn't succeed in making us chivalrous or preparing us for much that would come later in life, it was fun and I wouldn't have missed out on any moment of it or the weeks of camping that came later with Boy Scouts and Luther League.

Early Romance

When a person is young and starting out, a romance that ends before its time is viewed by the participants as tragic, but when a person is older, that same romance gone wrong may in retrospect seem amusing, pathetic, impractically unrealistic. With the distance that comes from time passing, we chalk such attachments up to experience, categorize it as puppy love, a relationship simply not destined to last, just one of life's adventures. The wound heals and there's barely a scar as a reminder.

My teenage years in Barron, a garden or orchard of delights, yielded some fruits of romance, some easily forgotten, some bittersweet, and, in a rare instance or two, romance without compare. Phil too tasted the apple. Popular in high school, as a junior he was voted Sno-Ball King and got to reign with lovely Queen Sylvia Thompson on a decorated throne in the festive gym. Because as Lutherans we didn't dance, that year the royalty didn't lead the crowd to the throb of the music then in vogue, but the dance at which they were feted marked time with the beat of Eden. At sixteen Phil was smitten by Judy Wiegen, the daughter of the owner of the Clover Farm, a vivacious brunette, witty, and a year and a half younger. They were a spirited pair, enjoyed each other's company, and relished sharing puns and good times at the local haunts.

The autumn of my sophomore year, while seated in the gym for an assembly, a pretty blonde freshman caught my eye. A few days later, having found out who she was and where she lived, I got up the courage to introduce myself to her. Her name was Kathy Sleugh, and she lived in the country near Prairie Farm and rode a bus with other newcomers to our high school. Kathy! I relished saying her name to myself and boldly out loud when I was alone. "Goodness gracious! Great Balls of Fire!" She consented to go on a date with me and a car full of others to Huffy's Hut in Cameron.

At Huffy's Hut, we'd sip sodas through straws, feed the jukebox, and joke and talk. Downstairs was a bowling alley. We'd take turn setting pins, no automatic pin setters then and, apparently, no worries by the management of liability issues. We weren't charged rental for shoes when we agreed that one of the people in our party would set pins. We'd be issued a large rough sheet of paper with squares printed on it to keep track of our frames and everybody's score, noting with whoops of delight any spares, strikes, and rare turkeys we bowled, minus any gutter balls. The pleasure of bowling and just being out with a person of the opposite sex whom we just barely knew but were eager to become friends with was exhilarating.

We'd get a little nervous at those moments when we chose to advance on the physical side. The daring step of slowly putting an arm around this person as we sat there together at a movie or a football game caused the breathing to quicken and sent a shiver through the body. And then the first kiss ventured. Would she move her face to deflect my approach or gracefully, almost intuitively cooperate, and meet me half way? Much beyond that had to wait till I was older and surer there was mutual abiding interest and longer term prospects for romance at stake.

Heather Townsend, whom I kissed at the door and, foolishly, not sounding sincere, declared, sort of experimentally, that I loved, became one of those memories you don't cherish. Crushes and infatuations when I was younger, however, continued to float through my daydreams later on. Barbara Shaide, a tomboyish girl who lived a block and a half from our house, was a flirt and a pal at the same time. I was one—I'm sure—of a dozen lucky ones who got to catch her and kiss her on the cheek when she—deliberately, I think—stumbled running away after leaving a May basket for me and ringing the door bell. It was extra fun when she joined us in a tramp through Thompson's Woods or helped build a cart or a snow fort. To be near her was a kind of pre-dating experience for us as pre-teenage boys. A few years later, Larry Stokes, who had moved to Barron to join us in second grade, confided that he had gone all the way with Barbara, and, though we didn't believe him, we asked him to give us the details. Linda Tabor, not quite so hoydenish but nonetheless palsy with boys, we'd play jacks or jump rope with. Being with her was a latently sensual experience. Though we were youngsters and playmates, she stirred fantasies in my mind when away from her company I happened to revive the memory of an innocent touch on the leg, arm, or back while playing tag. It was thrilling to participate in the coming of age with boys and girls whom we had known, gone to school with, and played ball and hopscotched with since kindergarten. Once east (or any direction) of Eden we can look back but never return.

Wheels

The wheel was invented long before my boyhood in Barron but its application reached a zenith then. I don't remember being in a baby buggy or on a tricycle, having moved to Barron just before turning six and in time for the tail end of kindergarten. But my first bicycle sticks in my mind. Unless a kid was rich that first bike was likely to be second- or third-hand. It might be a hand-me-down from an older brother or a bike that parents were disposing of for a son who had gone off to college and was, therefore, exclusively into cars. I got my first bike at eight and struggled till my legs could handle the twenty-six-inch-er. It had belonged to a distant relative who had acquired it well before he served in the army in World War II. It had a seat that was sort of a scaled down version of the seats seen on early military motorcycles, handlebars that swept out like a waxed moustache, and spokes, hubs, and sprocket corroded with unremovable rust. We gave the gift a new paint job and bought a sheep's wool cover to hide the obnoxious seat. My pride of ownership dwindled, however, when other kids outright joked about the relic.

Next year we junked it, and I upgraded to my brother's late- model Hawthorne. For his birthday, four days before mine, he had gotten a nice red-and-black used bike from Gamble's, the two-tone colors being the store's trademark.

Two years and four days later, after combing the ads for a month or more, my Dad and I drove off to Amery to buy a maroon and cream Monarch, which I kept till we moved from Barron when I was fifteen. It had a chrome headlight, a sturdy kickstand, a chain guard that didn't rub, whitewalls, a fine comfortable black leather seat, and panels concealing the frame bars. The back fender had a couple scratches but sported a large built-in reflector. It was not an object of ridicule but a ride many others coveted. Its New Departure brakes held up beautifully, even under the strain of the long coast down the steep hill into Taylors Falls the day we completed a trip that earned us a biking merit badge to sew on our Scout sashes.

On bikes we raced and roamed all over. We could be to the park and back again in barely half the time it took to walk from our house to the Skelly gas station on the corner of Highway 8, cross the street, and reach the tracks a block and a half this side of the park's west entry. Bikes accelerated our time to do stuff, and we were able to pack in a lot more adventure, not being limited to places we had to walk to or hike to to get to.

Living, we discovered, speeded up with wheels. Roller skates got us living so fast we had to keep a supply of band-aids handy. A drawback to them was that unless we tied a piece of yarn to the special key we needed to keep the skates clamped tight we'd lose the key and then have to contend with loose skates and the consequences when they flew off upon hitting a section of uneven sidewalk. At the roller rink in Rice Lake we had shoe skates. If we fell on the smooth floor, there was justification for embarrassment.

Wagons, scooters, and cobbled together carts all made their début. We didn't have the money to own a fleet of different wheeled devices, so scratch the scooter. Two or three times at most I got to ride a scooter. It belonged to Joel Edson, who was four or five years my senior. It stood idle in Edsons' garage, just kitty-corner from our house, when I was at an age it would have been great to have it myself. I got up the courage to ask to borrow it, but my pride got in the way of repeating the request. Besides that, we were busy making and racing carts. No motors, they were pushed with a sawed off broom handle. We used our feet to steer the two-by-four that served as the front axle and swivelled on a bolt in the middle. Bent over nails didn't do it, as we had learned after a nasty accident and upon getting tired of the repairs that held up our fun. The carts were all wood but for the wheels. If we wanted to get elaborate we'd nail on a peach crate to serve for a hood, using number-ten can lids to simulate headlights, and a smaller crate for a trunk. Doll buggy wheels had to be sneaked away and put on in private, else the girls would have had a fit. Genuine cart wheels with ball bearings were available at the Coast-to-Coast hardware store. But who could afford to buy them? Only guys whose dads wanted their sons to win a Soap Box Derby. We were doing this on our own. Dad was busy in his study, out calling, or over at church in a meeting. Besides, we had enough trouble heading him up for dough to go to the show. We had to improvise.

At the west end of Barron, just before the welcome sign for incoming traffic that read BARRON, INCORP. 2,319 POP., stood Peter Fox Manufacturing, later to be merged with the main turkey processing plant that has since become known nationwide. If we followed the railroad tracks, behind the building we'd come to a field that was graveyard for a few junked implements and vehicles. It wasn't a real salvage yard like the one Manors owned a mile east of the city limits. So it had no commercial value and no fence surrounding it. We'd stride through the tall weeds and hop onto a rusty tractor and push pedals and shift gears as if we were on the move. The chassis of an unrecognizable model of a pre-war automobile had gone to its final rest there too. A ways off lay the body, burned out, windows and upholstery gone, fenders dented, hood and hinges seriously damaged. The dash board still enclosed most of the instruments but the speedometer had been pillaged along with the cigarette lighter. Some promising things were still on the chassis: an in-line six-cylinder motor

85

with two of its spark plugs intact and the wires, carburetor, and cracked battery on the ground. The steering wheel and column had not been removed, and if we sat on the crinkled wire that was all that was left of the seat, we could spend precious afternoons driving anywhere in the USA— without using a drop of gasoline! But that luxury ended when we jerked the wheel off and took it home to grace the best cart yet in Barron.

Too young to drive legally, we did the next best thing. We joined the Manor boys at their dad's auto salvage for our own personal demolition derbies. We'd siphon gas out of other wrecks and, two to a car, take turns driving. We'd select a couple of beauties to whine, snarl, and skid round the dirt track that encircled piles of wrecks and heaps of memories. We learned a lot of mechanics—we had to—in the process. Cannibalizing batteries, tires, and other essentials, we didn't make money for Mr. Manor, but we got familiar with the locations and parts and could assist him when he was stumped by some arcane request of a customer who would try to dicker him down to get the part for next to nothing. The Manor boys were dare-devils. Phil and I did out best to keep up with them. On a dare once we all spent a night in the cemetery across the road from their fenced salvage yard, till our ghost stories got too graphic. In the wee hours, we trooped back with our sleeping bags to the house to proper beds.

Phil turned sixteen before we left Barron and promptly (April 24, 1955) got his driver's license. A few days later, for ninety-five dollars and fees, he titled over into his name a two-door 1941 Ford. It was black, as were most of Henry Ford's pre-war vehicles. But we customized it by adding yellow rear fender skirts, having louvers stamped in the hood, purchasing a kit to lower the car three inches, and installing dual exhaust with Hollywood glass-pack mufflers that produced a mellow roar barely within the range considered legal for street use.

Mom taught us how to drive when we were a few years younger. We'd take turns driving on blacktop or gravel country roads, and she did her best not to be a backseat driver. We thought we were keeping a secret from Dad, but it turned out he didn't object to our learning to drive so early but just wasn't available to help instruct.

As might be expected when brothers were so close as Phil and I, even though it was his very own car and the novelty of driving legally would take many more miles to wear off, he extended the privilege of the driver's seat to me once in a while. Mostly I rode shotgun but when we had a car full I'd join buddies in the back. We had a close call in Rice Lake once when I was behind the wheel. I slowed down at an intersection and, instead of coming to a complete halt at the stop sign, pressed in the clutch and slid the gear shift into second and purred on through. Right then from the opposite direction a police car came into view. By the time the cop got through the intersection and turned around, Phil and I had exchanged places. He took the rap and we split the fine. My name didn't appear in the newspaper. His did. I felt deep guilt and remorse for having sullied my brother's clean record. After that run-in, he wasn't so quick to invite me to take over at the helm, and anyway I decided I had better lay low. I postponed my driving career till our move to Iowa, where I got my license on my sixteenth birthday.

Old People

W e made a distinction between "old people" and "grown-ups." Grown-ups included our parents, other children's parents, and people their age plus or minus a few years. Grown-ups were "adults," a term in our recognition vocabulary but never spoken by us. Admittedly, grown-ups were much older than youngsters and could rightly be regarded as oldsters, but we invariably referred to them simply as grownups and reserved the term "old people" for the really old. Grandpas and grandmas, naturally, belonged in that category. But there was a whole race of people whom we considered ancient and labeled old people. The sort of men and women consigned to the rest home, distorted figures who couldn't hear, see, or walk much anymore.

Five old-but-still-nimble old men and one strange old lady in Barron jump instantly to mind. None ready to retire to the rest home, four of the old men lived alone in their own houses. The fifth was married and had an aged but spry wife. That couple also lived in their own house. And the strange old lady was cooped up in an old house that might just as well have been a cell in a madhouse or a prison. We could tell they were old by their gray hair, their wrinkled and spotted skin, their shaky voices, and the way they bent even when standing.

Mr. Alexander still drove. He had a '38 Plymouth coupe that I wished I owned. He had a small bean field that I was asked to help with. He had heard from the Broadbents, where we chiefly did our bean picking, that I was a serious worker. He called, and my mother agreed I would go. He picked me up in his coupe mornings and drove me to his place where I picked for several days. I brought my lunch, which Mom had packed, and would eat it in a shed by the field. The doors didn't shut tight so I could see even without opening them what he had stored inside. On my last day I asked him if he'd sell the airplane propeller I discovered there. I could hardly believe it. Mr. Alexander gave it to me. Phil and I planned to refinish it, install a clock in it, and mount it on our bedroom wall. According to Mr. Alexander it was from a World War I French fighter plane. I could make out the letters Nome engraved in the wood, but that didn't solve the mystery. Mr. Alexander had gotten the propeller from a fellow who had cut it to shorten it for use on a boat he sailed on the surface of ice. Clipped, it was still almost seven feet tall. I forget how much I got paid for the beans, and I don't know what happened to the propeller, which Phil and I never got time to restore. I think maybe it went with the other stuff we had stashed in the attic that Mom and Dad had to get rid of when we moved away. In my mind I can still picture Mr. Alexander's Plymouth with its wonderful floor shift, so many times had I dreamed he had decided to give it to me to save till I was old enough to reach the pedals and drive it.

Old Martin Foss, the man with a not-so-old wife, was hired by the church to paint the storms and screens at the parsonage. He'd arrive in a Model T, which made a series of little not-very-loud explosions. It went *pup-pup-puff*, pause, *putt-putt*, pause. He used a crank to start it. A white-walled spare tire of large diameter on a wooden-spoked rim and a luggage rack took up the rear. Mr. Foss roped a ladder and a pair of sawhorses to the roof. Good thing he was tall because Model T's are slung high, not low as Model A's were (even before being chopped and channeled for hot rods). To get into the vehicle—I almost said horseless carriage—Mr. Foss and any passengers had to step up on to a running board and pull themselves up by grabbing a leather loop that swivelled from the top frame inside each door. The interior was upholstered with fabric and tufted like a fine davenport.

Mr. Foss would set up shop in our garage and systematically paint all the sashes and screens and, with a wood mallet, chisel Roman numerals in them as if they were a set. Adroit with a putty knife, he'd reglaze a window in minutes. I liked the smell of the turpentine and the Dutch Boy oil paint which he swore by—not at—and took care to avoid spilling or splashing, though his bib overalls were no longer solid white.

Another unforgettable old man, whose name now escapes me, lived on the east end of town. He had a dray service and used a regular old horse to pull the wagon. He took throwaway items to the dump to discard, unless it was stuff he could salvage and sell. We hired him once to haul away old chicken wire Dad was afraid would be too bulky to transport in our car the next time we went to the dump. I can see them now, the team he and his horse presented, as they plodded through town. His conversation with the horse went well beyond the standard staccato commands of "Giddy-up" and "Whoa." We thought we heard him making civil inquiries as to the horse's welfare. He never used a whip and wouldn't stoop to mere clicks and grunts when addressing his horse. The horse was his pride and joy. They both seemed to enjoy the dray business, as if they had made a mutual career choice years and years ago.

An old man on my paper route was a veteran of the Spanish-American War. Despite his age, he would consent to participate in local parades but did so as a distinguished passenger in one of the several convertibles rounded up for the occasion. No legionnaire, Boy Scout, Cub Scout, or fireman could come close to the venerable old soldier in the degree of respect paid them by the spectators. The mystique he generated was unmatchable. And I got to deliver his *Evening Telegram*! He mostly muttered, owing to his age and long association with a pipe, so I did not get treated to any eye-witness accounts of the War of 1898. I always examined carefully the coins he handed me when I collected for the paper in case I'd be lucky and get a rare one to add to my coin collection. If that were to have happened, I guarantee I'd have forgone a show to preserve it.

In a house directly south of the alley behind the Farmer's Store lived a woman for whom time stood still. My mother would visit her and, one time, allowed me to attend her. Miss Havisham I'll call her, for I cannot recall her name. What I do remember vividly, however, is the time-warp experienced upon entering her house. The picket fence enclosing the lawn harkened back a half century as did the gingerbread trim on the porch—all with barely a trace of the original white paint. Inside one would think the place was a museum. Instead of electric lights Miss Havisham had kerosene lamps and a gas chandelier. A wicker rocker, a Victorian sofa and companion chair, tables and furniture adorned with doilies, fringed drapes on the windows, and heavy velvet curtains on rods in the archway separating the living room from the dining room, a woebegone grandfather clock gnawing away minutes as if famished from waiting for company, and a clutter of turn-of-the-century photographs—everything defied the future and held fast to the past. A recluse, the old lady (Mom had informed me in advance) had lost her groom (no one knew how) on the day of their wedding, and she never got over it. She all but quit living. Over the years she pined away. Except for my mother and the boy from the Farmer's Store who delivered her groceries according to a list she would post on a rust-free nail on her front door, she refused to have visitors.

If one only scratched the surface of Barron one wouldn't know how deep it was. In the foreground sunshine prevailed but in the background here and there amidst golden but now faded triumphs lurked shadows from life's little tragedies.

The Family Circle

G athering and assimilating trickles and traces of water as it flows along, a mighty river gains strength and unity from its tributaries whatever their size. The particular water that joins the general current adds to the magnitude of the river into which it blends to share purpose and direction with the current. So with a household, where each family member contributes to the whole, home life can nourish the spirit of each individual and collectively become an entity greater than the sum of the members who comprise it.

Some families, or leftovers of families, survive despite drought conditions, others perish when the waters of love and unity recede. In Barron I knew kids who, it was reported, "came from broken homes." We felt sorry for them. Oh, they were normal and all, but they lacked the refuge we took for granted. It was worse than having a broken bone, an injury that was temporary and with a cast and time would heal. Steve Jensen's parents were divorced. Steve lived with his dad, and his sister lived with her mother. A welder, his dad was great and seemed determined to make it up to his son by taking him hunting and fishing and giving him a weekly allowance, spending a lot of time with him because he lacked the advantage of having a whole family. But others didn't have it so good.

Fortunately, in our home each member of the family and, by extension, close friends whom we drew into the family circle, counted and helped make up the sum. For each of us children growing up, home was a place of loyalty, warmth, and identity, a source of comfort and support. Home was a bulwark, a place to return to when things didn't work out elsewhere that day. Except when we declared the intention of running away because we were scolded harshly and felt unappreciated in the family. Even then home didn't figure as a prison in our disturbed little mind. Rather, we were venturing out alone into a harsh world and accepting hardship not simply because we felt sorry for ourselves but because it was a means of getting back at the household so that those remaining could not be happy either. Apart or together the family was everything that mattered.

Mom read stories to us from *Grimm's Fairy Tales*, *The Arabian Nights*, and other children's classics as well as the Bible. We had phonograph records of stories too, among them "Sinbad the Sailor," "The Irish Washer Woman," and "Goldie Locks and the Three Bears." She also sang songs while she played the tunes on the upright piano in the living room. A special treat was when she continued to play after we had been tucked in our beds upstairs. I'd lie there and wait till my turn came again to hear her lilting, "O, Danny Boy." Sunday nights traditionally culminated in cocoa and toast around the dining room table. Mom always used the orange Fiesta ware pitcher to pour the cocoa from. All other times the pitcher sat in one of the corner cupboards with china that was removed only for dinners on Sundays and holidays. We felt like royalty, princes and princesses, at court at those times the family gathered around the dining room table and feasted.

Carole, who was a year and a half younger than I, and I were called "Love Bugs." We were great pals. I don't remember that we scrapped much at all in our family. In fact, we were envied by friends who didn't get along with their brother or sister or who were an only child and didn't have ready-made opportunity to play with children nearly their age right at home. All five, "The Five Little Peppers," as Mom

93

called us, would play Monopoly or work puzzles together for hours. Phil and I had to make a replacement "board" for Monopoly, when it divided into two worn pieces from constant folding. We made it out of plywood so it would endure. Every one knew the properties in order on all four sides, from Baltic to Park Place. We changed the rules so that no one would have to leave if bankrupt. We'd allow loans or partnerships to keep us all going. Caroms and both versions of checkers, Chinese and standard, were nearly as popular.

On a rainy spring afternoon, or while a blizzard raged in February, or any evening after homework was out of the way, Phil and I would retreat to our bedroom. There we would lie on our backs on our bunk beds and go through the countdown before our jet engines catapulted us into space. All kinds of gadgets and odd items from a "junk drawer" served as dials and switches for our make-believe rocket roaring off at a zillion miles per hour. We would communicate between top and bottom bunks by an imaginary transmitter. It could be a flight as far off as to the moon, a mission no one at that time thought possible. But the imagination has no boundaries.

The favorites at birthday parties were Spin the Bottle and Pin the Tail on the Donkey. Later, in Luther League we graduated from musical chairs to Wink'em. In our house, real cards were forbidden but Old Maid, in a deck that took no guesswork to avoid getting the Old Maid, and Authors, with Charles Dickens and Nathaniel Hawthorne leading the pack, substituted admirably. Calling on our dexterity, Tiddly Winks and Pick Up Sticks engrossed us for hours as well. On the theatrical side, we'd perform skits and make puppet shows. We devised scrolls with scenes that we unrolled, frame by frame, to the delight of the household. Why would we want to leave home or seek other companions when our family was a center of fun?

ॐ • ॐ

Trips to Minneapolis

We traveled to Minneapolis a lot. We had relatives there and had lived there for a few years before moving to Barron. Usually a trip to the Cities was made to visit the cousins or to shop. Dad's purpose in going there was educational. He took history and humanities classes at the university. Our teachers had no problem excusing us. First, we were excellent students and would not miss much or would readily make it up. Second, they were under the impression that our education was advanced by such trips. We would see and experience new things. We in fact enjoyed telling the teacher and our school mates about the event. And it is true that on the way home Dad would summarize the lecture he attended that afternoon. Words like "philosophy" and "hieroglyphics" would pop up as we passed Burma Shave signs and as our eyelids drooped after a day of excitement riding escalators and elevators and staring at all the people and all the merchandise in the Cities.

We could count on Mom to buy us chocolate stars, jelly beans, and nuts as treats to enjoy while we shopped and to tide us over till we had a late lunch at the Forum, a black-and-white marble-and-chrome cafeteria. We felt like dignitaries when we were seated at our private table with white cloth napkins, heavy silverware, glass tumblers, and china plates heaped with fare we had personally selected. We were limited to one dessert but could have as many vegetables as we wanted.

The twins were too young to benefit from the experience and Carole declined any offer to take a trip, for she got car sick as soon as we exited town. To idle away the time in the car, we would have contests to see who could see the most cars and trucks of a certain color or we'd see how many states we could rack up from out-of-state license plates. Sometimes we'd work a puzzle that had the alphabet scrambled. It was a maze and took a long time to put the letters back into order. Or one of us would say, "I'm thinking of . . ." while the others fired questions and guesses to narrow it down. The person who finally got it would then think of something and the questions would start over again. Besides billboards, every so often a sequence of Burma-Shave signs diverted us from asking how much longer.

We had this custom when we entered Polk County. Whoever saw the sign first would poke the others in the car, usually with a quick jab of the index finger to the ribs, and exclaim, "Polk County!" One time Dad poked me too enthusiastically, and I cried and said it was "too hard." He defended the "touch" but said he was sorry if it had hurt me. Maybe I was mad at not being faster and was trying to be dramatic. For a few minutes I pouted but I began to feel ashamed and turned cheerful again. I worried that my overreaction to the incident would cause a pall to be thrown over the tradition, and we would no longer engage in competitive "Polk-ing." Fortunately, next trip entering Polk County went fine. Everybody got their pokes in, one person the winner, and nobody a sore loser. Dad did go a bit lighter from then on, I noticed.

When we traveled to Minneapolis to visit the cousins, all of us went along. Carole would be granted a window seat and a packet of her favorite things for riding—paper dolls, colors and a coloring book, and one of Mom's spare purses to play grown-up. The rest of us, but once in a while including Carole, would vary the routine by switching from one car game to another. Once at the cousins', conversation, play, and eating intensified.

In our family and among relatives talk was fast and loud. We all got very animated in company. With so many present in such a confined area as a living or dining room, we had to pipe up to be heard. So too, with a large group around the table, we couldn't be bashful or we'd lose out there as well. If we left hungry or remained silent we weren't quick enough on the draw.

Girl cousins outnumbered boy cousins. Compare Kathy (called Kappy) and Kay and Carole, Christie, and Connie with Bob and Phil and Dan. Dad wasn't the only one who got his hard C's mixed up in trying to label each girl correctly. It was a challenge for anyone, even at slow speed. But Dad, who led the pack in velocity of speech, even mixed up the boys' names when he got going. It didn't matter though. We always knew whom he meant. And he usually corrected himself by adding the name he had intended to retrieve but in the rush of talking hadn't taken the time to pause to get it right the first time.

One of the novelties of getting together with relatives was to hear our parents called by their first names. When the cousins said Aunt Marky and Uncle Prop it was acceptable, but obviously we wouldn't use their first names ourselves. For the Substads it was the reverse when the Van Tassel children spouted Aunt Ardis or Uncle Arn. When the Substads visited us in Barron, conversation and play occurred at the same high speed. Topics varied, as did activities and places to romp, but the cast of characters and the script didn't differ.

ജ • ര

Weapons at the Ready

A ll quiet on the western front. We listened and heard no further noise of defense. We had routed the enemy. We were infantry, but not foot soldiers. We had crawled, like the Marines invading Normandy, on stomachs and hands and knees over the weeds and level land except where we bumped into a stump or an object like a rusty bucket or old warped board that had been tossed out in the field to get it out of the way. Such items we had to take care to watch out for, because they could be unexploded shells. This was no vacant lot; it was nearly a half block of open land, on the east end of which work had begun on a basement that would support a new house or one moved in to add to our neighborhood and subtract from our battlefield.

We felt mixed. The loss of valuable terrain was offset by the introduction of the steam shovel, a clanking monster that scooped out dirt by giant sized shovel loads to prepare for the construction of the basement. It had finished its task but sat there for weeks to rest and allow us to climb up on it and pretend to be doing things. Next came the cement mixing marathon when the wood forms were filled to the brim with oozing wet gray mud that hardened like rock so that when the carpenters tore down the forms the basement stood solid. We tested it by walking around the top, kind of scary because the center was a big deep hole and the sides hadn't been tarred and filled in yet.

One time Dick Kirkwood fell off to the outside and had to be yanked up from the dirt, but he didn't let it bother him. He strutted back up the plank crossing the chasm and got into the balancing act again, like a circus acrobat who misses the trapeze, plummets to the net, and immediately climbs back up the ladder to resume the act. But Dick had no tent-full of amazed spectators to delight, not even his parents present to cheer him on. When the carpenters started nailing up the shell, we watched and listened with fascination. When they broke for lunch we joined them to ask questions. They seemed to enjoy our interruptions and one time made us all sets of stilts from two-by-fours.

Our wars were not conducted only in Europe but out in the Wild West as well. Instead of wooden rifles rigged with a clothes pin to shoot bands cut from auto inner tubes or loaded b-b guns, we used cap guns or squirt guns to go after cattle wranglers or defend ourselves from attacking Indians. Such skirmishes could take place anywhere and didn't always require that we had a gun. We could use our fingers and point and trigger for pretend. And for a horse, all we had to do was slap our thighs with our hands. A favorite site for cowboys and Indians was the livestock pavilion down by the depot. When cattle were corralled there for an upcoming sale we had the added effect from the sounds and smells. We took turns being cowboy or Indian; it didn't matter. What did matter is that others took us at our word when we shouted, "I got you!" Victims rarely argued; they were supposed to fall down dead, at least for a minute or so. Then it was fair game again. Sort of like cartoons in which the creatures get killed and re-killed.

On nights when the town siren went off for black-outs, a drill for possible attacks, we got into the swing of things. From the platform of our tree house in the elm in front beside the driveway we'd toss paper sacks full of water down on kids below in the dark. It was almost as though they felt defeated if they didn't get splashed. We'd hear them squeal, "I'm soaked!" or "That one hit me square on the head!" We used a pulley and rope to pull up refilled buckets and made sure in advance to have plenty of sacks so we could double-line them.

In our double-decker tree house in the back, way up in a walnut tree, we'd perch and enjoy the view. Below was our chicken coop. The chickens roosted in branches of the lower trees along side the walnut tree till Dad put chicken wire across the top of the fenced-in sides. From up there we were level with rooftops and got a totally different perspective on our house and the lawn and garden. The clothes lines looked like telegraph lines, the basketball hoop looked odd because it was like we could have made buckets by dropping the ball rather than shooting it up to the rim or backboard. We saw the top of the plum tree and not the area where the trunk spread out and became roots and where we played with cowboy and cattle figures Mom brought back from her trip to the Mayo Clinic. In the backyard on warm summer mornings Phil and I and Mom would eat glazed doughnuts for early breakfast, Mom having made a trip to the bakery to surprise us.

We dragged our sleeping bags up the wood slats nailed to the trunk and slept up there one night. In the daylight we'd not only enjoy the view but would thrill at the distance a stone or walnut would fly from up there. We cut a bike innertube, removed the valve stem, and pounded a roofing nail on each end, stretching it between two upright limbs, to create a grand slingshot. To stay out of serious trouble we never aimed directly at a person or car in firing range. One time from a hiding place behind the hedge that ran along the Mill Street side of our house we threw plums at cars going by and got into trouble. A driver whose car we hit also got a plum through his window. He stopped and parked and went right to the door of Dad's study to report our mischief. Dad had us apologize to the gentleman and promise not to throw plums again.

Even for peace time it would have been great to have a horse or a pony. I always wanted one but never got one. I came close a couple of times, though. Once in Minneapolis I entered a contest at Dayton's to win a horse if the name I put on a slip of paper with my name and telephone number was chosen as the name for Roy Roger's new puppy. I printed Barrel on the piece of paper, thinking that a suitable companion to Trigger, the name of his horse. Some one else thought of the name Bullet, which won that person the colt. I guess I didn't sense that the part of a gun I nominated would suggest that the dog was big and round more than fast. Anyway, I lost.

When I was about thirteen, I had another scheme. Mom had an old school friend who had married a rancher in Montana. I got the address from her and sent her a letter expressing my interest in horses and my desire to get on as a ranch hand. The reply was friendly enough but dodged the issue. Perhaps they thought I was too young to do much good on the ranch. I had to settle for hanging out at the pony rides at carnival time. Twice back then we visited Uncle Bob Klanderud, one of Mother's two brothers, who lived on a small ranch outside of Sioux City, Iowa. Phil and I would admire the tack and horses in his stables, walk around the white-fenced race track, linger in the corral, and, when we got a chance, ride with Uncle Bob in one of the sulkies. A hired hand let us help pitch hay into the stalls. If we didn't have to go to school it would have been just the ticket to remain there on a permanent basis to assist with stable chores and help train and ride the horses. But truancy was a crime we weren't ready to commit. Maybe if school had been a drag for us as it was for some of our friends, we'd have made the move, assuming all parties had been willing.

It wasn't that I was constantly pining to have a horse. Get a pea shooter or a yo-yo into my hand or a kite or the Remington bolt-action .22 that I bought when I was fourteen, and I'd forget entirely that I was a horseless boy to be pitied. On or off the battlefield, on or off a horse, with or without, we rarely indulged the luxury of boredom. In Barron our options were infinite.

Life's a Spectacle

Phil and I had gone along with Mom and Dad on the trip to Pike's Peak, but we missed out on the high point of their trip to Canada. Of all the sites they visited, Castle Loma, in Toronto, took the cake. It was as if we were there, so clearly did the slides they took show what they saw. After Dad showed us the slides a number of times, providing a commentary as we shifted from picture to picture, we had everything memorized. And so we took over. Not when they were around and could have easily responded to our request to see the slides of Canada again. When they were gone for a half day or a couple of hours, we helped ourselves to the boxes of slides, the screen, and the projector. The familiar slides popped into view, one at a time, as fast as our fingers could load and unload the mechanism, inserting one on the right side while the one being shown occupied the center, then sliding that one out to show the slide that was loaded, at which time inserting a new slide. It was a slow process but we got deft at it and fewer and fewer times showed a slide upside down. We'd shut the Venetian blinds, pull the drapes, turn off the lights, flick the switch on the projector, focus the lens and move the table on which we placed the projector to help better focus the image. When we were rushed for time we'd skip the screen and show pictures on the wall, which produced some amusing variations, especially in the contour and size of the humans but also in the architectural integrity of the buildings.

Once when we thought we had ample time to go through the trip, rotating persons for commentary on each slide, we saw the headlights flash against the front window as Dad and Mom returned and pulled into the driveway. In my haste to fold up the screen, a heavy structure with spring action, I caught my right index finger in between the steel edges and gashed it. We might have kept the secret of our private show but for my wound, which required explanation and stitches. Surprisingly, Mom and Dad had no objections to our clandestine showings, even found them cute, so we had guarded our secret for naught. And I could just as well have collapsed the screen in a timelier fashion and spared myself a scar.

When we didn't want to go through the entire rigamarole of setting up and dismantling the projection equipment we could use a View-Master. We didn't check the batteries systematically so we couldn't count on its being bright enough to show the slide distinctly and would have to supplement the light by holding the thing up to a lamp. The show would be very slow motion, however, because it took time to pass the View-Master along to others who took interest in the slide we were viewing. Either their interest was sparked by the comments of previous viewers or their curiosity was aroused by the silence in which those viewers observed the slide. One way or the other everyone was bound to be included in the viewing. That's why we usually set up for a family viewing, sans parents. Now and again we'd plan a show in advance and invite friends over. We charged no admission. They must have thought we did a lot of traveling as youngsters, given the authority with which we glossed each picture on the screen.

Like the View-Master but not for pictures of people, places, or things, a kaleidoscope was another source of delight for the eye. Phil got one as a Christmas gift, and we all got repeated turns with it. No image was ever the same. Just like no two snowflakes are identical. Any jiggling, any deliberate turning of the lens, any adjustment to the light, any change of angle, and, of course, any different subject matter (color and texture and size) made a difference. We couldn't be sure when we tried to share a particular view that the person who looked next saw anything close to the one we had ooh-ed and ah-ed over. How different from looking at most ordinary things or even, say, the stars. Point out the Big Dipper and everybody could easily find it even later on. But a kaleidoscope created its own world every fraction of a second, every shift of the hand.

When the carnival came to town, we'd go to the Penny Arcade and see Peep Shows. They were brief and comical. It was hard to share them because by the time we let a friend, or he let us, see, the show had progressed and it didn't make sense for either of us.

Telescopes and binoculars were fascinating too. When we saw a squirrel way up close it looked more human than animal. It was about impossible to keep a flying bird in view through binoculars. It was hard enough when they perched up in the top of a tree because then we were trying to separate the foliage from the bird and whether we looked through the lenses with both eyes or squinted and used one eye, the image would be as steady or shaky as the hand holding the binoculars.

Now, a magnifying glass was another chance to distort our views of things. Hold it up to an arm and the skin was all pocked with pores and freckled. Insects were instantly monsters. But one thing endlessly fun about a magnifying glass was how fast we could set a leaf afire and smoking by aiming the beam of sunlight on a spot of its surface. It was hard to believe the sun was ninety-three million miles away when we could call on its energy just like that.

Another strange perspective was when we looked through our parents' glasses, which they depended on to read and drive, and see how blurry everything became. Assuming that the prescriptions were correct, we almost couldn't imagine what they saw without their glasses. Maybe they saw the blur without them that we saw with them. I don't know. I didn't want to stare too much through them or I'd be sure to get a headache or, worse, become permanently cross-eyed.

An elderly couple who were parishioners gave our family a stereoscope. We had been enthralled by theirs when we visited their house one Sunday afternoon for dinner and talk and, in this instance, entertainment. A stereoscope did in black-and-white and single images what 3-D movies do in color and flow, once we put on the special glasses. The photographs on the card we inserted in wire bands down the end of the stem were doubled. When we peered through the eyepieces we felt convinced that we could reach out and touch the scene. It was so real!

A periscope and the opportunity to swim would be the main reasons I'd join the navy, if I were to choose whether to go army, air force, or navy. But I'm pretty sure I'd find submarine duty claustrophobic. The novelty of the periscope would probably wear off soon, and unless I were in the South Pacific, the water would probably be too cold to enjoy swimming. Besides it was a lot more fun and handier to play war close to home.

Photo albums were good and bad. It was a drag to have to look at old wedding pictures and family reunions with relatives who were no longer alive. On the other hand, seeing grown-ups when they were babies or children our age made them seem more like us. It cut them down in size, which was a little embarrassing but quite amusing.

Old automobiles and forgotten styles of clothes were curiosities. Men in military uniforms all looked important and reminded me of Boy Scouts, except we had fun and, by the looks of it, soldiers didn't enjoy what they were doing, whether it was being shot by a camera or by real guns. Anyway, I'd sooner work a complicated puzzle than try to figure out who all the people present in a group photograph were—their names and what they did and how they were related to us.

One time my dad drove Phil and me out to the edge of the golf course road way late at night to see a lunar eclipse. Another time he prepared smoked glass for us to view a total eclipse of the sun. We could be blinded if we looked directly at the sun. Some people used a shoe box with a hole poked through both ends to catch the shadow effect. But we thought Dad's method gave a better view. Those with the shoe box probably don't remember the event, whereas for us it was indelible. Dad always was a fount of knowledge about things, whether lore related to nature or facts about how the ancient Greeks lived and what they thought. One time Dad took us down the basement to watch him skin a dead rabbit, showing us how to keep tugging the skin back without letting any fur touch the meat part. He had grown up on a farm, though it was hard to tell that from the way he dressed. He mostly wore suits, starched white shirts, ties, and wing-tip shoes. He almost always wore a hat, never a cap. Even way back in the photo albums, we'd see him dressed up, though there was one picture of him wearing overalls and a cap when he was maybe nine years old and the future didn't appear to concern him in the least. When our family went on vacation or a picnic, he'd wear a sport shirt, flannel if it were chilly. Some people knew him only as the Reverend and saw him almost exclusively in his clerical collar, robe and surplice, and stole. That's surely the image that Rodney Olson, as a towheaded tot, beheld when identifying Dad's office as the residence of God Almighty.

There are many angles from which to view life, and the lenses we looked through provided perspective while they distorted. We wondered if any two persons ever saw things exactly the same way.

Daredevil, Adventurer, Pioneer?

Columbus, the Pilgrims, Benjamin Franklin, Robert Fulton and Thomas Edison, Daniel Boone and Teddy Roosevelt, Harry Houdini, Charles Lindberg and Amelia Earhart, Babe Ruth, Emily Dickinson, Frank Lloyd Wright, Evel Knievel and Elvis Presley— American history is replete with examples of the spirit to press beyond conventional challenges, the desire to expand the boundaries of human knowledge and experience, the goal to discover lower depths and higher heights. In the roll call of American originals are instances of the marvelous and the ingenious. Some of the mighty are deserving of columns in an encyclopedia. Others are owed an entry in *Ripley's Believe It or Not* or the *Guinness Book of Records*. A portion are granted a niche in one or another of the halls of fame.

But for every adventurer whose name becomes history, there are hundreds, perhaps literally thousands, of unsung heroes. Every town boasts runners-up. They get celebrated locally and become part of history, lower-case "h." Runners-up die and are buried in obscure cemeteries in tombs that might as well be designated for the unknown or little remembered citizen. It is a commonplace that every human being is unique and possesses a spark of the divine. Each and every one of us yearns to dream the impossible dream. In short, adventuring is innate to humankind.

Not recorded in the annals of human history are countless deeds of daring, remarkable exploits, undertaken by everyday boys and girls and ordinary men and women. In Barron, for instance, there are many accomplishments I can attest to that could have made history except that no one was present to publicize the events or the persons who turned such moments into events. An irony here is that many a person has invented a wheel or whatever that someone else who hit upon it earlier got the credit for. An individual's independent creativity is misjudged as dependency, and people are said to be copiers or plagiarists just because they didn't do it first, never mind that they did it without coaching and not by imitation.

We credit Ben Franklin with the discovery of electricity. His experiment with a key on a kite is well known. Tons of children have flown kites since that day, perhaps even a few with a dangling key instead of a tail made of knotted-up nylons. I believe that all children's kite flying gives them proximity to greatness. That activity puts them in the league, minor or little as it may be, with such legends as Icarus and Wilbur and Orville. The kiting part, the flight part, we all can relate to. As to the electricity part, all children have either explored household outlets to the point of being shocked, rubbed their feet on carpets and touched others with static power, or created sparks by flipping a wool blanket in bed after the lights are off. Each of us discovers electricity but we give Ben all the credit. Shocking as it may sound, the fact is children have been discovering electricity all along, before Ben, after Ben.

Isaac Newton is credited with formulating the law of gravity. Yet we know that apples fell before his time. And after. Sigmund Freud is acknowledged for his findings regarding human sexuality. But we know that the modalities of experience he studied and discoursed on predate his experiments into psychoanalysis. What I'm saying is that we all have a touch of greatness, but while our possession of a share of such greatness may imply equality, it doesn't imply superiority. That bit of greatness we possess in common with all others is an entitlement that does not and will not earn us the greatness that history accords those "greats" who first stirred the attention of significant others by their discoveries. We have to be content with, or at least resigned to, our obscurity, however akin we feel to those who have achieved fame. What connects us all is the urge to do something spectacular, something we and, so far as we know, others haven't done before, that something involving a high level of risk. We dare to try.

We don't settle for the vicarious; we want to experience things for ourselves. A farm is a wonderful place to experiment. There we are thrown back in time to the roots of our being. There we can gain an appreciation for the life cycle and the food chain. In such an environment we come to understand or intuit the principle of survival of the fittest. On a farm we see the harnessing of natural and mechanized forces for the betterment of civilization.

Electricity and power machinery have transformed farming. Over time cattle have been herded into enclosures. Walls of stones and fences of wood and iron have done their part to keep animals in captivity. The saga of the West is tied to steel both by the iron rails that united the Atlantic with the Pacific and by the development and adaptation of barbed-wire fences. Horse farms in Kentucky are outlined with beautiful white wood-rail fences. A simpler fence began to dominate the Midwestern farm at mid-century. In came the electric fence. Cows didn't need to get zapped more than once or twice to learn to stick together within the pasture and not to yield to the temptation to see and nibble the greener grass on the other side of the wire.

Intrigued by the current pulsing through the wire, we boys had to check it out for ourselves. Unlike the bovine experimenters, we would not desist from touching the live wire after an initial shock or two. Our persistent contact with the electric fence was not based on our being dumb animals or Pavlovian failures. Rather, it was predicated on two counts: number one, it was generated by "I dare you"; and, number two, it was motivated by "I'll give you a dime if you can hold on while I count to ten." Man, or in this case, boy, is a higher order animal. He lives by his wits and by the sweat of his brow. Jolts from holding on to the wire are not lethal. They are not therapeutic. They are exciting. They demonstrate one's courage. And as the enterprising lad jingles coins in the pocket, the jolts become remunerative. Clearly, it is a win-lose-win arithmetic, any way it's figured. Taking bets on the challenge of withstanding electric charges for a given length of time wouldn't make for a rags-to-riches story. It wouldn't match what a kid could make by the sweat of his brow in the bean field. But for the short duration it paid well by the hour, though here we're talking seconds more than even minutes of "work."

Though I did not later draw on these moments of firsthand knowledge of electricity for my report on the REA, I benefited by accumulation when the need came for ready cash to buy such Thoreauvian necessaries as fish tackle, a whistle, or a Mars candy bar. A criminal can rob a bank but if caught could pay for his unrealized pleasure by going to prison, maybe even to the electric chair. My payment was small in comparison, and I got something to show for my bout with electricity. This was the first publishing of my discovery of the wonders of electricity. The profit from it got me to Ben Franklin's Five-and-Dime, across from the Barron County Court House.

Earlier Sir Isaac Newton and the effects of gravity were noted. Again, as a boy growing up in proximity to farms, I studied and participated in laboratory exercises propounding the benefits of gravity. I and three other young Newtonians—a.k.a. my brother Phil and Richard Degerman and his brother Russell—dared to defy gravity's force, when we undertook to roll down hill on a hay wagon at Degermans' farm. The experiment would reveal whether the turning apparatus, namely the hefty tongue of the wagon, could be held up by twine so as not to impede the wagon's progress and acceleration, and still permit a measure of control when used as a steering device. Furthermore, it would show whether the ride down the inclined plane could gather momentum such that the experimenters themselves might have cause to bail out or would instead persevere, keeping true to the "dares" they as Newtonians had shared amongst themselves before boarding the platform, and thus complete the experiment by trial and error to verify or nullify the hypotheses noted before engaging the wagon and while surveying the terrain that was proposed for traversing. The results were stunning. The craft did not get hung up by the tongue but the steering was inexact and consequently the craft, against all predictions, ran into one of the poles propping up a 100-gallon gas tank. Fortuitously, the impact rather than upsetting the tank and precipitating a much greater catastrophe, only bent one of its four supporting legs. Sir Richard had bravely averted danger by giving the command to jettison while he cranked the tongue to the right enough to deflect a full frontal collision before jumping off himself.

When Farmer Degerman was informed of the experiment and its mixed results and came out to inspect the site, he was at first nonplused. Quickly gaining composure, he uttered, "Dad blame it, my gosh, how'd you do it!" His marvel at our scientific feat had a worrisomely ambivalent note to it, one that bode no great future for us in the Pickwick Club. His comment was the swan song to our unsung heroism that day at the farm. But our adventures and discoveries weren't over. They simply took another turn, away from the ominous gas tank and toward other potential obstacles.

Economies

Living in "America's Dairyland," as noted by the slogan emblazoned on the state's license plates, and growing up in a county that celebrated its dairy industry by local festivals, one would assume that milk and milk products were readily available and cheap. After all, the entire countryside was given over to herds of dairy cows and farms were everywhere. Why then did our family not stay content getting milk from the milkman who delivered door-to-door all over town? Well, Mr. Mulligan lost his job when he was discovered to have juggled the books to pocket more than he should have from his customers. He overcharged us, and we quit taking milk.

Rather than simply picking up our milk at the grocery store, which we did for a spell, we explored a more economical source. The Barron Cooperative Creamery sold, bulk fashion, a type of milk, which was said to be skim milk. It was the liquid left over after the cream was churned into butter in large vats. We were issued a couple of two-gallon glass jugs to carry and store the skim milk in. I don't know how much it cost, but we were told that it was a lot cheaper and just as good as any milk we got from the milkman or bought at the store. The problem was that it didn't taste right. Not that it was sour. I've drunk sour milk and even buttermilk, which Mom used to make doughnuts and pancakes. The "milk" we obtained from the creamery was bluish white and had yellow flecks in it, probably fat that didn't get turned into butter, we guessed. I blame the creamery. It was one thing for them to sell off their excess steam to the high school and any businesses that desired to buy their heat that way. But for them to capitalize on what was left over from their butter making was going too far. In our quest to economize, we became victims.

I wondered how Dad found out in the first place that they had this stuff for sale. It was wretched. I hadn't minded our not buying homogenized milk. Mom would pour off the cream at the top of the bottle to save to use for whipping cream, for cooking, and to cool and flavor hot coffee or cocoa. Once in a while we could have cream on our oatmeal or, more rarely, in a bowl of freshly picked raspberries. Regular milk tasted good. But what we got from the creamery wouldn't make us want to ask for another graham cracker to dip. We wouldn't be needing more to wash down chocolate chip cookies or to swill when cleaning mashed potatoes and vegetables off our plate. We protested and, finally, won out, Dad's protestations of LTA ("learn to accept") notwithstanding. In his surrender speech, he declared that we were pampered and should think of the starving millions in China who'd be glad to have even a sip of what we turned up our noses at. A new milkman took over the route, and we resumed business as usual. I felt a renewed sense of patriotism.

The best treat of all was to squirt milk fresh from the cow into our mouths. I about said "faces," since it was hard to focus the stream immediately at the lips. We'd splash ourselves till we got it aimed right and got the hang of it. It was warm and creamy and rich right from the cow's bag. It hadn't been tanked yet in the cool water, and it hadn't been filtered, processes that were all part of the farmer's twice-a-day chores.

Another attempt by our family to economize on the dairy end involved butter and the butter substitute, known as—here we best whisper—margarine. The only margarine permissible by law to sell in

Wisconsin in those days was a non-yellow (that is, non-butter looking) vegetable-based spread that came in a clear plastic bag. It didn't look like butter in shape either because it didn't come in a pound block or in quarter-pound sticks in cartons that could be made into train cars or May Day baskets. Inside each bag lodged a red bean that Mom (or one of us boys) could cause to explode when she (or one of us) squeezed the bag at that end. Then she (or the delegated kneader) worked the bag like putty till the red dye mixed with the whitish margarine to turn it first orange around where the bean was and then yellow throughout to resemble butter. Word was that in Iowa people could get pre-colored margarine. But of course this was Wisconsin, where there was a lot riding on the dairy enterprise. We felt a little guilty when the clerk rang up the margarine at the checkout counter. We weren't patronizing the state's mainstay commodity. We stuck to butter, however, for places where its absence would otherwise be sorely evident, say, on toast, waffles, bread, lefse, or johnnycake. It wasn't so critical an ingredient in general cooking and could, thereby, help with the grocery bill.

I liked going with Mom to the grocery store except it sometimes seemed to take too long. Going to the barbershop was another matter. I loved every minute spent there: the time watching and listening to the wall clock, the time spent reading *Field and Stream* and *The National Geographic* while waiting for my turn, and, especially, the minutes it took to complete the haircut. I felt important on that pumped-up, cushy chair. While I wasn't in it for a shampoo and shave, I still merited the undivided attention of the barber. He would ask me questions and tell me things as if I were the main attraction. Preparations began with the stiff paper collar he'd tuck down around the cloak wrapped around me to keep the shorn hair from sticking to my clothes. For twelve minutes, while I watched the minute hand of the clock gradually move, he'd buzz the clipper up and down and back and forth, flicking tufts of my hair to the cloak where they'd slide to the floor, sometimes with the help of a little nudge from one of my arms hidden below. He'd click off the warm clipper, and with a long-tapered comb in one hand and a shiny scissors in the other he'd do the final touches around the ears, across the forehead, and along the back of the neck. A second later, he'd grab a curiously shaped, interestingly labeled bottle from the marble shelf beneath the mirror to wet my hair down for the combing, then swing my chair around for me to inspect and comment on the job. He'd defrock me, whisk off any loose hair, sprinkle powder on my neck, pump the chair down, and let me out. I'd thank him and give him two quarters. He'd remark, "That should do you till next time."

Outside, people noticed. They'd say, "I see you got your ears lowered."

We always got our money's worth by asking for a full haircut and not just a trim, as Mom had prompted us beforehand.

Once to save the fifty cents he'd been given by Dad to get his hair cut at the barbershop, Phil had me cut his hair. That time people really noticed. First off, Dad and Mom! Then the kids at school. I thought I could manage it. I had watched it being done to others and to myself. But the scissors didn't cut it the way the barber did. Maybe if I had a clipper it would have helped. If the haircut at home had worked for Phil, I was going to have him do mine. But we started and stopped with his.

When the price of haircuts bumped up a quarter, Dad tried to economize by having a fellow who lived a few blocks away and had a clipper cut our hair at half the price. Mr. Loukes might nick us once in a while and we didn't get the little extras we got from a professional but it beat what we could do at home. I can't say I enjoyed our move away from the barbershop. But money talked.

I don't know that Mom's sewing us clothes was principally a matter of conserving funds. She relished selecting and modifying patterns, picking out fabric, and making a garment that would fit and looked good. For Phil and me she embroidered Western shirts that made us feel and look like movie stars. The pockets, cuffs, and collars were outstanding, with closely stitched colored threads forming patterns that would have complemented the fanciest tooling seen on a saddle or holster. We hated to outgrow those shirts. The girls' dresses too were often homemade, either by Mom or Grandma Klanderud. We could count on the twins to have identical dresses, but there were times when Mom outfitted the trio in the same fashion. We have photos in the album to prove it.

When it came to getting clothes from rummage sales, however, the specter of economy arose. We felt embarrassed because the clothes usually didn't quite fit, in part because of having been worn from the start by other bodies they didn't rightly conform to our bodies. And wouldn't other kids suspect they weren't our clothes from the beginning? Else how is it that no one saw us in them when they were new but only now when they were worn? Granted, they were cheap and they covered our limbs and if we were in China we'd have been thrilled to have them. But I preferred clothes that were store-bought or Mom-sewed over someone else's hand-me-downs. Rummage sales were the yard sales of yesterday, everything looking so threadbare and obviously discarded. Could it be that we were clotheshorses back then and didn't know it?

Shortly after we moved to Barron, Dad, not a fan of Henry Ford, traded in the family 1937 Chevrolet for a 1946 Chevrolet, and later upgraded to a 1949 Chevy, a white "Golden Anniversary" model, in the trendy torpedo-style. But with barely six inches of clearance, it was not a car suited for rutted, snowy, country roads. It was continually becoming stuck and having to be pulled out by horses or tractor in the winter. Maintaining frugality, Dad had the engine overhauled twice at a local garage and got the body repainted by a farmer who did auto-body work on the side. The deep green version purred another hundred thousand miles of vacation travel, trips to the Twin Cities, and calls on rural parishioners, at whose homes he occasionally performed baptisms and weddings and served communion to shut-ins, those of the flock for whom getting to church was problematic even when there wasn't a blizzard. When the green car—green by virtue of color, not fuel consumption and carbon emissions—was retired for the last time, the new tread parked in the pastor's driveway supported a sporty bustle-back, two-tone blue-and-white '52 Chevy. By choice or budget, Dad never gave his vehicle business to GMC above the Chevrolet division. Furthermore, till Sioux City and the purchase of a plum-and-imperial-white 1956 Impala, all Dad's cars were used, not new.

I'm told Dad's dad, most of whose life predated automobiles, was more at ease with horses. On his farm outside Stillwater, he shoed horses and forged wheel rims, leaving it to old Henry to mind the automobile assembly line and to the younger generation to navigate mass-produced horseless carriages with trumped-up horse power motors and spoked rubber wheels. When Grandpa Van bought and drove his first Ford, he spun into the shed masquerading as a garage, bumped into the wall, and exclaimed, "Whoa! That'll stop ya now." Heading off to the Cities, he ordered Dad, just thirteen then, to take over the steering wheel, throttle, and brakes. Never mind licenses and insurance. In those days, too, pedestrians took liberty to hop onto the running boards and get a lift around town—an early form of hitchhiking or carpooling. Why walk or pay for a taxi when you could get a free ride?

While we had to economize in a number of ways, we never came close to starving. There was always plenty to eat, never any to waste. To re-quote Dad, WDS! We did not regard ourselves as poor. We knew people who were poor, and we pitied them. We realized that we were not wealthy. We knew people who were rich, and we envied them only when there was something they had that we wanted and knew we would not get. We felt numbered among the fortunate. Our lives were happy, and we wanted for nothing. The frugality that we grew up with was an asset not a liability. We balked at certain economies, but we did not resent the lifestyle we were granted. I cherished it then and cherish the memory of it now. Viva Economies!

Treble Clef

Linda Tabor and I were diagnosed as monotones back in third grade. I didn't hold it against the music teacher, an attractive young woman who visited Miss Heinline's class twice a week for an hour to provide enrichment. I had already discovered that I couldn't carry a tune. I take that back. I had no trouble singing along with a group, whether hymns or popular songs, so long as I could be led by others and, it really helped, when there was someone at the piano maintaining the melody. I was aided also by the location of the circle parts of the notes on the music bars. When they were low on the bars I'd go lower and when they were high I'd go higher. The business of singing parts was too much for me. I liked to listen to others bring all the respective parts together but in music I preferred to walk familiar ground and stay—and it wasn't always easy—with the melody.

When I was six I was trotted off to Miss Gyland's, three blocks west and a block north to a house on the corner of Division, to learn to play piano. My parents had joined the conspiracy of parents expecting their children to gain skill and, it was hoped, excellence on this most basic of instruments, particularly if it appeared the child wasn't going to have a career in athletics. Later on in high school we were either in the

118

band or on the court, or—because not every guy on the team plays—on the bench. What, otherwise, would end the pause parents would be caught in when other parents bragged about their child's athletic prowess or musical precocity and we didn't play anything? We'd let them and the whole town down. The best prevention was for parents to introduce the child early on to both arenas so that by hook or crook the novice would develop into a performer, be it music or sports.

Every Tuesday at four o'clock I'd head to Miss Gyland's for instruction. There were two Miss Gylands, old-maid sisters. Thelma, the younger and more energetic, worked at the Farmers' Bureau and served gratis as our Sunday School superintendent, an assignment she took and made others take very seriously. Martha, who had silver hair and always looked like she had just had a permanent, was more reclusive. She joined others at church on Sunday but didn't get involved in teaching Sunday School. During the week she preferred to stay at home, where she made a little income by teaching little fingers to play piano, John Thompson fashion. I could not really get the hang of it. The long strip she'd unfold and place above the keyboard to make more obvious which keys were what didn't do the trick. Nor did the half-hour practice sessions at home adduce to my progress. I never made it to "John Thompson's First Grade Book." I didn't even finish the one for "the earliest beginner." I got as far as "Song of the Volga Boatmen," at which point I threw up my hands, figuratively speaking. My repertoire included "Sandman's Near," "The Postman," and "Rain on the Roof." Not to mention the first work in the book, "Birthday Party," which served as my recital piece.

Miss Quiggly, our first-grade teacher, invited all her pupils to perform on a given day. Still sniggering over her name? Just to make it all the more funny, the name of our kindergarten teacher was Miss Wiggly. Wiggly and Quiggly. It's the truth! Anyway, Miss Quiggly's invitation led to my doing the selection "Birthday Party." When I was through with my performance, I strolled back to my desk, satisfied, even proud, that what I did would have pleased even Miss Gyland. But fate is not easy on a six-and-a-half-year old. Linda Elkin, who had been taking piano since she got out of her bassinet and, when it came her turn, graced us with a selection from an advanced John Thompson collection, lowered her head, wrinkled her brow, stared at me like a school principal, and practically shouted, "You didn't even start at Middle C!" *What did it matter*, I thought. Besides, I was pretty sure I had kept the spacing approximately in order. It was disappointing to have what I thought was a success criticized as a failure. My first and only public performance was a turning point for me. Within weeks I had persuaded my reluctant mother to set me free. No more piano!

My brother had all the talent. Invited to audition, he was chosen to be part of the newly formed Rice Lake Boys' Choir. We both had to be in the Children's Choir at church, though I probably did more damage than enhancement in that role and in the white robe which we all wore when performing.

In seventh grade I decided I would explore the instrumental side of music again but this time concentrating on a wind instrument. Maybe I was a late bloomer and the talent I and others hadn't seen or heard when I apprenticed on the piano would now surface and surprise all my classmates, including Linda Elkin. I signed up for trumpet lessons. The band leader at school issued me a rental to get started. Two lessons out and what had I learned? Don't puff my cheeks out like a hamster when blowing a wind instrument. I struggled to make a sound that resembled music, not a vulgar noise that only made my lips sting. I had been supposing I would be a natural and nothing would stop my advancing to a young men's drum and bugle corps. I was sorely mistaken. I wasn't willing to sacrifice valuable time that could be better spent doing lay-ups, shooting free throws, and practicing dribbling in exchange for drilling to be able to march in precision and carry a tune at the same time. Better hoops than toots, I concluded. I threw in the towel on music and cast my lot for junior high basketball.

Oh, I didn't give up altogether. I still enjoyed singing around a campfire, going caroling, belting out rounds at camp (where everyone could count on me for an enthusiastic rendering of "John Jacob Jingleheimer Schmidt"), and joining in on familiar hymns at church and Luther League. With hymns like "Rock of Ages," "I Love to Tell the Story," and "Onward Christian Soldiers," popular hits like "Cruising Down the River," "I Love Those Dear Hearts and Gentle People," or "I'm Looking Over a Four-Leaf Clover That I Overlooked Before," a few Negro Spirituals adapted by Stephen Foster, songs from the musical "South Pacific," and most of the Christmas Carols, I could do my part, I mean do my share. I might have been a monotone but I wasn't a freak. I noticed at church others had difficulty too when the organist picked a seldomly sung hymn. It often resulted in an organ solo. Maybe that was her intent.

Plus, I was able to bang out elementary tunes along with other members of my family on the xylophone Aunt Bertie had given us. Dad could play a jews' harp and a harmonica and had no trouble carrying a tune. He even composed a hymn when he was in the seminary. The girls weren't monotones. And Mom—bless her heart!—was an accomplished vocalist as well as a pianist. She played and sang mostly by heart, though she read notes like a professional when learning new pieces. Her services were always in demand at church doings. She sang in the church choir, often sang solos for weddings, and sang over the radio, on WJMC, a couple of times. I was the black sheep when it came to music. The most I could offer was a bleat or a blare, by voice or by horn, unless, as I said, it was a familiar tune. I was a decent whistler, though.

To tell the truth, in eighth grade I nearly failed "Choral"—me, a straight-A student. I know it didn't help that I whispered during rehearsal, but out of class I made a point of buttering up the teacher so I wouldn't create a scandal in town. "Did you hear that Reverend Van Tassel's son flunked music?" Fortunately, I worked on my P's and Q's and got E, G, B, D, F and Middle C figured out and as well made improvements in how I comported myself during rehearsal. I succeeded in averting a crisis. My report card that term didn't have to be presented to my parents in shame.

Lest I be thought hopeless, I should add that there were times when I sang a cappella, with no other voices and no accompaniment. Such singing was not restricted to times in the bathtub but could take place whenever or wherever I was completely out of earshot, maybe on a solitary tramp through a neighborhood or up at Olsens' farm. I didn't turn up the volume terribly loud. In fact, sometimes I didn't actually sing out loud but rather imagined I was singing. I won't say I was singing to myself because in my fantasy I had an admiring audience, occasionally a single listener, only a beautiful girl listening intently and longing for my lips to become silent and form a pucker and meet hers.

Once at a talent show I got inspired when a young man in a costume sang "Old Man River" in a baritone voice. After my voice changed, I thought I might be able to improve on his performance by singing that song in a bass voice. I practiced it on some of my jaunts in case I should get the courage to enter the talent show some year and wow the local audience from the stage overlooking the courthouse. But that never happened—in Barron or elsewhere.

ॐ • ॐ

A Calendar of Surprises

T he element of surprise, not the kind of surprise that can shock or threaten but the kind that picks up the spirits, is important to our pursuit of happiness. Happiness can't just be turned on by the exertion of will power. Happiness isn't only the result of having achieved a goal. It can arise from something not of our own doing. It may come out of nowhere, as a stroke of good luck. It may be the manifestation of consideration by another party. A surprise can (indeed is usually intended to) bring pleasure at a time of stress or when things seem jejune and unpromising. It might take the form of an uplifting message from a far-away friend, a bouquet arriving at a time of confinement, an unexpected treat like the announcement of a reward or an activity not planned but suddenly a reality. A surprise is having things turn out better than anticipated, as in the case of a comedy, which typically ends by wiping away all fear and doubt and animosity and, in a welcome but not so predictable reversal, by celebrating union and understanding, for the characters on the stage as well as for the audience. A surprise is a gift rather than something earned. It is bestowed on a recipient who, till then, isn't expecting to receive anything. Otherwise, there's no surprise. Children's lives are visited by surprise after surprise. Surprise is an attitude.

When we let fall out what may, when we are in the prevailing mode of adventure, replicating the perspective of the child, we are likely to encounter surprise after surprise. For, when we know or think we know too much, the element of surprise shrinks, and then when it does arise it may be mistaken for irony. Because we are caught off our guard, it may have the effect of humiliating us. It's salutary for adults to be reminded at times that a grown-up's ken doesn't account for all things. A sense of wonder should reside in us all, not just in children. When we deprive our imaginations, the world of surprise and wider opportunities vanishes, and we lose valuable prospects for happiness by living in such a diminished world. The same holds true for humor.

When I look back to a calendar year as a boy growing up in Barron, I recall being daily "surprised by joy," to summon a phrase and a concept from the poet Wordsworth. The condition of surprise was by no means perpetual but it was dominant. In retrospect, we can recapture that attitude and relive that experience by kindling the imagination and memory.

For a child, a calendar is a promise of days to come. On it holidays are marked out. Special events are penned in by Mom, perhaps a trip that is being planned or a birthday to be celebrated. We looked forward to these "coming attractions." February 4th, ten days before Valentine's, was the twins' birthday.

Spring was the season of family birthdays, Dad's on March 18th, Mary Jane's on the 22nd of April, Phil's on the 24th, and mine on the 28th; then Mom's on May 3rd. Mom and Dad's wedding anniversary was March 19th. Dad always said, "I was born one day and married the next!" It was one of those jokes we laughed at each time we heard it. Carole's birthday came in early fall, September 14th, shortly after school began. One other April birthday to celebrate was Domino's, on the 26th. Of course there were relatives' and friends' birthdays adding to the honors. We especially liked the fact that Domino shared in our close series of spring celebrations.

Just before supper on a day in early June, we trooped up to Fernettons, two blocks west and a block and a half south, adjacent to a pasture belonging to Olsens' farm, to see the litter of new-born puppies. Fernettons didn't plan to keep them all. Would we want to take one? Yes! It was unanimous. But, wait, Dad hadn't had his vote. We put dibs on one of the little puppies and returned home prepared to wage a campaign to add a member to our family circle. Surprisingly, we didn't have to launch a single argument. Dad instantly okayed the adoption. He acknowledged that Mops' disappearance a few months earlier had left a void. When we brought the five-week-old puppy home and placed him on a baby blanket on the card table, Dad exclaimed, "There's Domino!" He was black and white and small and going to be lots of fun. The name stuck.

Domino moved into our room and shared the foot of the lower bunk. Phil and I would dress him up in jeans and a jacket. Once we put him in pj's and tucked him in bed for Mom to see. When she came in a moment later to kiss us goodnight, she played the game and accepted a lick on her face from the dog. We'd feed him peanut butter and watch the action and listen to the snapping of his tongue against the roof of his mouth as he relished the treat. He was a swimming partner and accompanied us in boats, on hikes, and in the car. When we went "hunting," which turned out to be mostly target practice shooting tin cans off fence posts with BB guns or .22s, Domino tagged along. (Phil and I and Dad weren't into shotguns and preferred to see fowl in flight rather than in the bag.) Not a habitual roamer, Domino returned from a lone expedition one afternoon during the winter holidays carrying a frozen fish he had plucked from a wooden barrel display on the sidewalk in front of the Clover Farm Store. "There's nothing to do about it," Mom remarked. "Fortunately, it isn't road kill." She prepared the catch for dinner and rewarded Domino with an extra portion of dog food that evening.

The only consolation in having to part with Domino when we moved from Barron to a city, where he would have had to be tied out or taken on a leash, restraints he had never known and we didn't want to subject him to, was that he would carry on his lifestyle and adventures and be free to roam. His new home was a farm outside of Barron owned

125

by a "good Lutheran family" who were thrilled to adopt him. There are still photos of him in the family album. He was one of the best surprises Phil and I ever had.

On Easter we expected to get a basket as well as join in on coloring eggs. The basket would be a surprise. On a bed of green cellophane grass nestled a pair of dyed and decorated eggs, a variety of candy, and some small stocking stuffer type items such as a miniature car or truck, a little book, jacks and a ball, or a yo-yo. For May Day we prepared by making baskets from butter cartons cut in half and covered with crepe paper. We'd staple handles on them out of strips of colored poster paper and fill them with candy. The idea was to deliver the basket to a friend's house, ring the door bell or knock on the door, and then run. If the recipient were a girl, then we'd pace ourselves accordingly. We'd pretend to slip or act as though we didn't know that she was chasing. We'd slow down and appear to get caught unawares, so that she could plant a kiss on our forehead or cheek while she hugged us like a football tackle.

At Valentine's Day we made or cut out valentines and gave them to our classmates at school. To someone special we'd also give heart candy, the kind that had messages on them that were either gushy or funny.

Candy was part of every holiday, especially Halloween. We'd bring our hoard home, dump it all out on our area of the dining room table, compare our goodies with what came out of the bags of the others around the table, fondle it till our hands were all sticky, gloat over it as if it were a bag of treasure, sample generously, and before going to bed gorge ourselves, as we did the year before and as we would the next Halloween. It was the force of custom. "Trick or Treats, Money or Eats"—the chant was magical. In costume we were free to beg and take. On no ordinary night could we take such liberties or expect such generosity from folks all over town. We'd be on the alert for news from others in disguise as to which houses were handing out the biggest prizes. Then, because we couldn't make stops at all houses, we'd make a dash to those places where large candy bars were handed out with abandon to all comers, getting there before the supply or we were exhausted from the night's workout. Maybe at Christmas we would get a box of chocolate-covered cherries from one of our paper customers, but Halloween was the night we could depend on getting our bag and tummy filled with sweets.

Late summer could find us up in the limbs of an apple tree in a vacant lot across the street from where Karen Sandvy lived. We'd eat green apples till we were stuffed. They weren't the unripe or sour kind of green apple. These were choice. If we weren't in that tree or in our tree house at home, we might be doing as the squirrels, gathering walnuts to store for the winter. The one thing bad was that our hands started to stick together and turn black from the coating on the walnuts.

Another tree that captured our interest was the horse chestnut. The brown nuts with white spots made ideal rings and could be strung into necklaces. When roasted the chestnuts were more than decoration. Trees were friends and sources of adventures and play. We raided birch trees for bark to make toy canoes. Trees were great to swing from and to climb in. As Robert Frost noted and many an adult looking back would have to admit, "One could do worse than be a swinger of birches." In the glory that is childhood, we admired trees, whether standing apart from others and commanding the top of a hill or growing together in a woods or in a clump. They gave shade when it was hot in the summer and donated their leaves in the fall so we could build leaf houses, raking the colored leaves into rows to outline the rooms. Bobbing for apples and burning piles of leaves gave fall a taste and an aroma all of its own. Not to leave out the rustle of corn stalks and the smacking of corn on the cob. Pumpkin pie and jack-o'-lanterns rounded out our ode to Autumn.

Dandelions might be weeds but we found them useful. We could split their stems with our teeth, or, if we didn't want that bitter taste on our tongue, use our fingernail and they'd curl to both sides, like a topped fleur-de-lis. We'd rub a kid under the chin with the yellow flower to see if he or she were in love. If the patch where we rubbed turned butter yellow, that proved it. When the seeds were ready to go we'd blow the air full of them, and when they fell they would start an entire field full of dandelions. What daffodils were to Wordsworth dandelions were to us children—something to occasion a gaze in wonder and, if we wanted, to pick with abandon.

Tall grass blades became whistles when placed correctly between our thumbs. We'd fold our hands, press our lips against the thin opening between our thumbs, and blow. The sound resembled a muted trumpet. In a lawn of clover mixed with grass it didn't take more than ten minutes for one of us to find a four-leaf clover. At night, we didn't have to stare long—and often we didn't have to stare at all—to see a falling star. The world outdoors was magic, and it cast its spell on us from dawn to late at night, at least as late as we were allowed to stay out.

At times, edibles were available from the road. I certainly don't mean road-kill. Leave that to the crows. If an army convoy passed through town on Highway 8 we could stand along the curb and be tossed army rations. They were edible and said to be nutritious, but I wouldn't advise them for a regular diet. We got our fill of them at Scout Camp. When beauty queens on floats passed by in a parade they gave out taffy along with smiles. The candy beat the rations but of course wasn't supposed to substitute for vitamins, cod-liver oil, and plenty of vegetables. In mid-summer we could expect trucks loaded with peas on their way to the cannery to lose bunches of pea plants as they rattled by on Highway 25. We'd scoop them up and sit on the curb, busting open the pods and spilling the fresh peas into our mouths. There's no way they tasted as good cooked and on a plate at dinner time. The taste of harvest peas was unmatched, even by the different but equally good green flavor of the beans we'd wipe off on our pants and eat fresh from the field while picking for profit the last two weeks of the summer before school started.

Besides the treat of fresh vegetables and berries, we enjoyed picking red clover blossoms. They tasted like honey when chewed. No wonder bees are crazy about clover. Days we strolled to the park, we'd pull up a grass weed to suck and crunch on the way. Unless we had a pack of

Black Jack or split a piece of Juicy Fruit. Bubble gum would work and was fun for a while but soon lost its flavor and made our jaws tired.

Milkweed pods had shiny contents like feathers bathed in juice. When we cracked them open and allowed them to dry, the feathers would float off in the breeze. With cattails we could have fun too. Their fuzzy brown spikes would explode into the air when the plants dried out. Before they reached that stage we'd pick them, getting our feet squishy wet while grabbing their long stems and pulling them out of the marsh. We used them for torches, dipping them in kerosene and lighting them. Their stems made excellent handles. When we waved them, sparks would shoot up and fizzle. A long stemmed plant that I don't know what to call and that grew in abundance along the creek behind the creamery made good swords. They'd dry up and stiffen with the coming of winter. Through the snow we'd battle our way to school, replacing swords as need be from an endless reserve. As understanding as Mom was of the ways of boys, she occasionally queried us as to why or how it took so long to get home after school. But our damp clothes sort of gave us away.

One thing we never picked was trilliums, not a single one. It was illegal. Wildflowers we picked and presented to Mom included lilacs, roses, daisies, dandelions, violets, and bunches of fruit blossoms. Pussy willows lasted a long time when stuck in a vase with water. Plucked morning glories didn't revive after folding up at night; we might as well let them be. The largest and most brightly colored leaves were toted home where they could be admired by Mom or taken to school to show the teacher and add to her collection, some specimens finding their way to the bulletin board.

In October the color, scent, and shape of leaves was nature's show. A rival show came out of Detroit. Townsfolk would flock to the Chevy and Ford dealerships to marvel at the new models. After the interruption of the war, the auto industry got into a schedule of three years per model, with minor cosmetic changes annually. Then back to the drawing boards for an updated model for the next three years. Phil and

I became more observant of this cycle as we crept closer to the car zone in age and studied issues of *Car Craft*, *Hot Rod*, and *Motor Trend*. Chevrolet modified in a slightly altered sequence. The 1949 Chevy set the trend through 1952, with the option of a torpedo or bustle back style. Ford, however, with its boxy design inaugurated in 1949, broke pattern in 1952. Chevy put out a larger, new model with 1953 and 1954, and then let all the stops out in 1955, a classic to this day. Ford countered with the Crown Victoria. Both offered convertibles, Ford producing a retractable hardtop. Panoramic windshields, huge taillights, shiny grilles and chrome strips, V-8 engines, colored leather interiors, and spectacular dashboard instrument panels paved the way for the era of the Muscle Car. Corvettes and Mustangs and Thunderbirds set the style. Chrysler was more modest, its Plymouth taking a minor share of the market, till they rolled out the Hemi and the Barracuda in the sixties. Down on Division, Swant Brothers. showed off Oldsmobiles and, till they were defunct, Kaisers and Frasers. Like the Studebaker, Kaisers and Frasers were ahead of their time but lost out in the end. Packard and Nash beat them to the graveyard, despite the vitality they possessed in years past. In those days the brands of automobiles differed radically in design, and there was nowhere near the variety of models that emerged over the next several decades. Still, the fifties were in the vanguard of the automotive industry and foreign makes hardly made a dent or a ding in the hegemony of Detroit. People in Barron and all over the country made the pilgrimage to the local shrines come October. The invention of the wheel has had an interesting evolution, and we were on hand to witness some remarkable adaptations, including the mutant Edsel, with its horse-collar grille, which flopped because people then weren't keen on the retro look and preferred modern to post-modern. All manner of opinions were being voiced in the showrooms on October afternoons in the fifties. Things were astir in Detroit.

In Exeland, Wisconsin, a village of three hundred, north of Barron by some fifty miles, where we lived for a year after moving from Minneapolis and before landing in Barron, the spectator sport centered on the locomotive rather than the automobile. When the train puffed and chugged into the depot, people gathered to watch and remark. The coal car would be reloaded and soaked with water poured from the wooden tower tank that stood beside the track opposite the platform in front of the depot. The iron horse, branded Burlington-Northern, was powered by coal, not diesel fuel. It spit and choked and pushed and pulled and put people in touch with the rumblings of the Industrial Revolution. It was man's link with his fellow man, coming from other towns and cities and moving on to yet other towns, carrying cargo by the tons that only trains of snake-like length and rhythm could manage to deliver. A train's commercial viability as a conveyance of passengers also fascinated onlookers. Who were these people on the train? How could they afford to travel in such luxury and convenience? Where had they started their journey and what were their respective destinations? As the train clanged, rang, banged, and whistled to a halt at the station and hissed momentarily before clanking and wheezing on to the next stop, people stood in astonishment on the platform.

In Barron, the train wasn't the only show in town but it was still a show. Morse Code telegraph lines abuzz with dispatches, iron-wheeled wagons heaped with canvas mail bags, customers alighting from passenger cars or purchasing tickets inside the depot, mystery shrouding the whereabouts of the passengers and freight—all the same elements pervaded the atmosphere of the depot in Barron. I was a frequenter because of the *Evening Telegram*, which I relayed from the train to my customers by bike. My other link to trains in Barron was a memorable activity sponsored by our Cub Scout pack. We rode the train backwards to Cameron and then frontwards to return to Barron, there being no roundhouse or switching facility or time or need to point the locomotive the same way for both legs of the trip. We could double the feeling of going in reverse by switching to a seat that faced the rear. When we rode facing the rear while the train headed the other direction, the countryside appeared to be sliding away from us rather than approaching. On our ten-mile round trip we didn't get to try out a berth or sample the menu. But it was novel covering the distance by rail rather than foot, bike, or car.

Train tracks were part of the landscape. On treks out to Sandy Cliff, we'd tramp over the railroad trestle past Olsens' farm and walk the ties and the rails four miles to our favorite cookout site and source of fresh spring water. The route cut through the countryside. Here and there junked cars and retired farming implements were visible along the fences outlining the pastures and woods on the sides of the tracks. The faster we walked on the rail the better we balanced. When walking on the ties it was best to skip one and take two at a time, they were so close together.

Though we'd have been jailed should we have been caught, we flattened pennies on the track. Placing the penny when we could hear the train coming but before the engineer or conductor could see us, we then sequestered ourselves, lying low behind bushes. After the caboose whizzed by, collect and inspect the transformation. The penny was a thinner, wider copper wafer with a surreal trace of Lincoln's face and the minted letters formerly etched on the coin, now all flattened and, as the law warned, "defaced." I wondered then which was the more heinous, to deface or to counterfeit. We never dared counterfeit. And, believe me, we didn't make a steady practice of defacing currency. We didn't have coins to spare or money to burn. We had learned as children that money didn't grow on trees. We had to work for it. Which meant bean picking, delivering papers, mowing lawns, raking leaves, and shoveling walks. We could make a little from a lemonade stand or when Harvey Paulson hired us to peddle flyers door to door with that month's advertised specials. One day we made a killing waxing the Cadillac owned by a doctor and his physician wife who lived in one of the two haciendas in Barron, their lovely home a block south of our parsonage, and its counterpart, at the east end of town, the residence of Louie Olson. We didn't make much when we went door to door selling or taking mail orders for greeting cards, seeds, or—and we did it only once, because we had to for Scouts—bath and hand soap. We had our hands full delivering newspapers. Country kids, however, could sell a calf they'd raised and come into a fortune. Byron and Vernon Etlecker were always doing that. And they had a lot to show for it—hunting knives, hightops, nine-volt flashlights. Their dad, Rex, who was a giant of a man and who generously let us use their cottage on Prairie Lake, paid the boys handsomely for doing extra chores. One time they got a bonus when they and their dad triple-handedly pulled down an old silo with a heavy rope.

Whether it was the felling of a tree or a silo, the budding or falling of leaves, picking beans or eating windfall apples, the arrival of a night train at the depot or the display of new models of cars in the showrooms in October, events in Barron may not have gone down in history but they provided us a cornucopia of surprises.

Epilogue

I'm going reveal a little secret, a confession that won't spoil the visit we've had to Barron back in the 1940s and 1950s. It will simply put it into perspective. I grew up on the banks of the Amazon River! What? Yes, when my brother and I built and launched our first boat, we rowed it on the river, fished from it, used it as a diving platform, and circumnavigated the globe with it. Sometimes it was the mighty Mississippi, other times the Congo, one of the Seven Seas, or the Panama Canal (as described by Richard Halliburton in *The Book of Marvels*). We didn't just stay on the Amazon, of course. Humans don't stand still but are always on the move, responding to the restlessness borne of boredom or, as boys on the prowl for adventure, surrendering to the magnetic pull of the imagination, a kind of innate wanderlust. Frankly, it didn't matter then and it doesn't much matter now that the river was in fact the Yellow River, flowing through the farms and fields and towns of northwestern Wisconsin. For Phil and me it was all rivers!

The mind is a marvelous thing. It gives us the powers of observation and imagination. It expands our voyage through life. When we think about a port to set sail for, the imagination can keep us from thinking too small.

The realization that we can't literally go home again is a truism we must all eventually accede to. It is akin to acknowledging that the current of a river we're rafting carries us along so that the contour of the bank on either side is never the same and we are ever moving onwards, even at those very moments while glancing back to see where we've been. Yet our empirical sense tells us that when we look back, we somehow are there again. You can go home again, but only on the wheels of memory and imagination. To look forward is to have vision; to recall the past is to dream with our eyes open.

The Yellow River still flows today. Its waters aren't the same from one day to the next as always and yet it's one continuous movement of substance through space. The past is all we know for sure. We were there. Now we happen to be here but are thinking about there, where we have been. Bon voyage!

About the Author

Born in Minneapolis, Minnesota, in 1940, Daniel Ellsworth Van Tassel and his family—parents, brother, and three sisters—moved to the village of Exeland, Wisconsin, when he was four years old. It was his father's first call as a newly ordained Lutheran minister, and it involved serving a parish of four village and country churches. A year later, the family moved to Barron, where they lived for a decade before moving to Sioux City, Iowa, in 1956.

The author of this chronicle of growing up in rural and small-town America at mid-century earned his B.A. from St. Olaf College and his M.A. and Ph.D. from the University of Iowa. He taught at Concordia College in Moorhead, Minnesota; Chapman University in Orange, California; Pacific Lutheran University, in Tacoma, Washington; and, for over two decades, Muskingum College, in New Concord, Ohio, where he served as academic dean and professor of English. His scholarly publications include articles on Shakespeare, Hardy, Lawrence, and Beckett. Currently an adjunct professor at California State University San Marcos, he and his wife, Rhoda, also an academic, reside in Carlsbad, California, close to daughter Abigail, son Nathaniel Barron, and other family members.